Mastering Microservices with Java

Master the art of implementing microservices in your production environment with ease

Sourabh Sharma

PUBLISHING

BIRMINGHAM - MUMBAI

Mastering Microservices with Java

First published: June 2016

Production reference: 1240616

Published by Packt Publishing Ltd.
Livery Place
35 Livery Street
Birmingham B3 2PB, UK.

ISBN 978-1-78528-517-2

www.packtpub.com

Credits

Author
Sourabh Sharma

Reviewer
Guido Grazioli

Commissioning Editor
Veena Pagare

Acquisition Editor
Indrajit Das

Content Development Editor
Arun Nadar

Technical Editor
Tanmayee Patil

Copy Editor
Safis Editing

Project Coordinator
Ritika Manoj

Proofreader
Safis Editing

Indexer
Rekha Nair

Production Coordinator
Manu Joseph

Cover Work
Manu Joseph

About the Author

Sourabh Sharma has more than a decade of experience of product/app development. His expertise lies in developing, deploying, and testing N-tier web applications. He loves to troubleshoot complex problems and look for the best solutions.

In his career, he has successfully developed and delivered various standalone and cloud apps to happy Fortune 500 customers.

Sourabh has also initiated and developed a microservices-based product for his US-based top enterprise product company. He started writing Java programs in his college days, in the late 90s, and he still loves it.

About the Reviewer

Guido Grazioli has worked as an application developer, software architect, and systems integrator for a wide variety of business applications, crossing several domains. He is a hybrid software engineer, with deep knowledge of the Java platform and tooling, as well as Linux system administration. He is particularly interested in SOAs, EIPs, Continuous Integration and Delivery, and service orchestration in the cloud.

www.PacktPub.com

eBooks, discount offers, and more

Did you know that Packt offers eBook versions of every book published, with PDF and ePub files available? You can upgrade to the eBook version at www.PacktPub.com and as a print book customer, you are entitled to a discount on the eBook copy. Get in touch with us at customercare@packtpub.com for more details.

At www.PacktPub.com, you can also read a collection of free technical articles, sign up for a range of free newsletters and receive exclusive discounts and offers on Packt books and eBooks.

https://www2.packtpub.com/books/subscription/packtlib

Do you need instant solutions to your IT questions? PacktLib is Packt's online digital book library. Here, you can search, access, and read Packt's entire library of books.

Why subscribe?

- Fully searchable across every book published by Packt
- Copy and paste, print, and bookmark content
- On demand and accessible via a web browser

Table of Contents

Preface

Microservices architecture is a style of software architecture. With the introduction of the cloud, enterprise application development moved from monolithic applications to small, lightweight, and process-driven components called microservices. As the name suggests, microservices refers to small services. They are the next big thing in designing scalable, easy-to-maintain applications. It not only makes app development easier but also offers great flexibility to utilize various resources optimally.

This book is a hands-on guide to help you build enterprise-ready implementations of microservices. It also explains the domain-driven design and its adoption in microservices. It teaches you how to build smaller, lighter, and faster services that can be implemented easily in a production environment. It also gives you the complete life cycle of enterprise app development, from designing and developing to deploying, testing, and security.

What this book covers

Chapter 1, A Solution Approach, covers the high-level design of large software projects, the common problems faced in the production environment, and the solutions to the problems.

Chapter 2, Setting Up the Development Environment, teaches you how to set up the development environment, from the IDE and other development tools to different libraries. It deals with creating the basic project up to setting up spring boot configuration to build and develop our first microservice.

Chapter 3, Domain-Driven Design, sets the tone for the rest of the chapters by referring to one sample project. It uses this sample project to drive through different functional and domain combinations of services or apps to explain domain-driven design.

Chapter 4, *Implementing a Microservice*, takes you from design to implementation of the sample project. It covers not only the coding but also the different aspects of microservices—build, unit testing, and packaging. At the end of this chapter, a sample microservice project will be ready for deployment and consumption.

Chapter 5, *Deployment and Testing*, teaches you how to deploy microservices in different forms, from standalone to a container such as Docker. It will also demonstrate how Docker can be used to deploy our sample project on a cloud service such as AWS. You will also grasp the knowledge of microservices testing using REST Java clients and other tools.

Chapter 6, *Securing Microservices*, explains how to secure microservices with respect to authentication and authorization. Authentication will be explained using basic authentication and authentication tokens. Similarly, authorization will be explained using Sprint Security. This chapter will also explain the common security problems and their solutions.

Chapter 7, *Consuming Services Using a Microservice Web App*, explains how to develop a web application (UI) using Knockout, Require, and Bootstrap JS libraries to build the prototype of web application that would consume the microservices to show data and the flow of sample project—a small utility project.

Chapter 8, *Best Practices and Common Principles*, teaches the best practices and common principles of microservice design. It also provides the details about microservice development using industry practices and examples. This chapter also contains the few examples where microservice implementation goes wrong and how you can avoid such problems.

Chapter 9, *Troubleshooting Guide*, explains the common problems encountered during the development of microservices and their solutions. This will help you follow the book smoothly and make learning swift.

What you need for this book

For this book, you can use any operating system (Linux, Windows, or Mac) with a minimum of 2 GB RAM. You will also require NetBeans with Java, Maven, Spring Boot, Spring Cloud, Eureka Server, Docker, and CI/CD app. For Docker containers, you may need a separate VM or a cloud host with preferably 16 GB or more RAM.

Who this book is for

This book is intended for Java developers who are familiar with microservices architecture and have a reasonable knowledge level and understanding of the core elements and microservice applications but now want to take a deeper dive into effectively implementing microservices at the enterprise level.

Conventions

In this book, you will find a number of text styles that distinguish between different kinds of information. Here are some examples of these styles and an explanation of their meaning.

Code words in text, database table names, folder names, filenames, file extensions, pathnames, dummy URLs, user input, and Twitter handles are shown as follows: "You can create the `Table` entity using the following implementation, and you can add attributes as you wish."

A block of code is set as follows:

```
public class Table extends BaseEntity<BigInteger> {

    private int capacity;

    public Table(String name, BigInteger id, int capacity) {
        super(id, name);
        this.capacity = capacity;
    }
}
```

Any command-line input or output is written as follows:

```
docker push localhost:5000/sourabhh/restaurant-service:PACKT-SNAPSHOT
docker-compose pull
```

 Warnings or important notes appear in a box like this.

 Tips and tricks appear like this.

Reader feedback

Feedback from our readers is always welcome. Let us know what you think about this book—what you liked or disliked. Reader feedback is important for us as it helps us develop titles that you will really get the most out of.

To send us general feedback, simply e-mail feedback@packtpub.com, and mention the book's title in the subject of your message.

If there is a topic that you have expertise in and you are interested in either writing or contributing to a book, see our author guide at www.packtpub.com/authors.

Customer support

Now that you are the proud owner of a Packt book, we have a number of things to help you to get the most from your purchase.

Downloading the example code

You can download the example code files for this book from your account at http://www.packtpub.com. If you purchased this book elsewhere, you can visit http://www.packtpub.com/support and register to have the files e-mailed directly to you.

You can download the code files by following these steps:

1. Log in or register to our website using your e-mail address and password.
2. Hover the mouse pointer on the **SUPPORT** tab at the top.
3. Click on **Code Downloads & Errata**.
4. Enter the name of the book in the **Search** box.
5. Select the book for which you're looking to download the code files.
6. Choose from the drop-down menu where you purchased this book from.
7. Click on **Code Download**.

You can also download the code files by clicking on the **Code Files** button on the book's webpage at the Packt Publishing website. This page can be accessed by entering the book's name in the **Search** box. Please note that you need to be logged in to your Packt account.

Once the file is downloaded, please make sure that you unzip or extract the folder using the latest version of:

- WinRAR / 7-Zip for Windows
- Zipeg / iZip / UnRarX for Mac
- 7-Zip / PeaZip for Linux

The code bundle for the book is also hosted on GitHub at `https://github.com/PacktPublishing/Mastering-Microservices-with-Java`. We also have other code bundles from our rich catalog of books and videos available at `https://github.com/PacktPublishing/`. Check them out!

Errata

Although we have taken every care to ensure the accuracy of our content, mistakes do happen. If you find a mistake in one of our books—maybe a mistake in the text or the code—we would be grateful if you could report this to us. By doing so, you can save other readers from frustration and help us improve subsequent versions of this book. If you find any errata, please report them by visiting `http://www.packtpub.com/submit-errata`, selecting your book, clicking on the **Errata Submission Form** link, and entering the details of your errata. Once your errata are verified, your submission will be accepted and the errata will be uploaded to our website or added to any list of existing errata under the Errata section of that title.

To view the previously submitted errata, go to `https://www.packtpub.com/books/content/support` and enter the name of the book in the search field. The required information will appear under the **Errata** section.

Piracy

Piracy of copyrighted material on the Internet is an ongoing problem across all media. At Packt, we take the protection of our copyright and licenses very seriously. If you come across any illegal copies of our works in any form on the Internet, please provide us with the location address or website name immediately so that we can pursue a remedy.

Please contact us at `copyright@packtpub.com` with a link to the suspected pirated material.

We appreciate your help in protecting our authors and our ability to bring you valuable content.

Questions

If you have a problem with any aspect of this book, you can contact us at
questions@packtpub.com, and we will do our best to address the problem.

1
A Solution Approach

As a prerequisite, I believe you have a basic understanding of microservices and software architecture. If not, I would recommend you Google them and find one of the many resources that explains and describes them in detail. It will help you to understand the concepts and book thoroughly.

After reading this book, you could implement microservices for on premise or cloud production deployment and learn the complete life cycle from design, development, testing, and deployment with continuous integration and deployment. This book is specifically written for practical use and to ignite your mind as a solution architect. Your learning will help you to develop and ship products for any type on premise, including SaaS, PaaS, and so on. We'll primarily use the Java and Java-based framework tools such as Spring Boot and Jetty, and we will use Docker as container.

 From this point onwards, µServices will be used for microservices except in quotes.

In this chapter, you will learn the eternal existence of µServices, and how it has evolved. It highlights the large problems that premise and cloud-based products face and how µServices deals with it. It also explains the common problems encountered during the development of SaaS, enterprise, or large applications and their solutions.

In this chapter, we will learn the following topics:

- µServices and a brief background
- Monolithic architecture
- Limitation of monolithic architecture
- The benefits and flexibility microservices offers
- µServices deployment on containers such as Docker

Evolution of µServices

Martin Fowler explains:

> *"The term "microservice" was discussed at a workshop of software architects near Venice in May, 2011 to describe what the participants saw as a common architectural style that many of them had been recently exploring. In May 2012, the same group decided on "µServices" as the most appropriate name."*

Let's get some background on the way it has evolved over the years. Enterprise architecture evolved more from historic mainframe computing, through client-server architecture (2-tier to n-tier) to **service-oriented architecture (SOA)**.

The transformation from SOA to µServices is not a standard defined by any industry organization, but a practical approach practiced by many organizations. SOA eventually evolved to become µServices.

Adrian Cockcroft, former Netflix Architect, describes it as:

> *"Fine grain SOA. So microservice is SOA with emphasis on small ephemeral components."*

Similarly, the following quote from Mike Gancarz (a member that designed the X windows system), which defines one of the paramount percepts of UNIX philosophy, suits the µService paradigm as well:

> *"Small is beautiful."*

µServices shares many common characteristics with SOA, such as focus on services and how one service decouples from another. SOA evolved around monolithic application integration by exposing API that was mostly **Simple Object Access Protocol (SOAP)** based. Therefore, middleware such as **Enterprise Service Bus (ESB)** is very important for SOA. µServices is less complex, and even though it may use the message bus it is only used for message transport and it does not contain any logic.

Tony Pujals defined µServices beautifully:

> *"In my mental model, I think of self-contained (as in containers) lightweight processes communicating over HTTP, created and deployed with relatively small effort and ceremony, providing narrowly-focused APIs to their consumers."*

Monolithic architecture overview

μServices is not something new, it has been around for many years. Its recent rise is owing to its popularity and visibility. Before μServices became popular, there was primarily monolithic architecture that was being used for developing on premise and cloud applications.

Monolithic architecture allows the development of different components such as presentation, application logic, business logic, and **data access objects (DAO)**, and then you either bundle them together in **enterprise archive (EAR)/web archive (WAR)**, or store them in a single directory hierarchy (for example, Rails, NodeJS, and so on).

Many famous applications such as Netflix have been developed using μServices architecture. Moreover, eBay, Amazon, and Groupon have evolved from monolithic architecture to a μServices architecture.

Now, that you have had an insight into the background and history of μServices, let's discuss the limitations of a traditional approach, namely monolithic app development, and compare how μServices would address them.

Limitation of monolithic architecture versus its solution with μServices

As we know, change is eternal. Humans always look for better solutions. This is how μServices became what it is today and it may evolve further in the future. Today, organizations are using agile methodologies to develop applications; it is a fast paced development environment and is also on a much larger scale after the invention of cloud and distributed technologies. Many argue that monolithic architecture could also serve a similar purpose and be aligned with agile methodologies, but μServices still provides a better solution to many aspects of production-ready applications.

To understand the design differences between monolithic and μServices, let's take an example of a restaurant table-booking application. This app may have many services such as customers, bookings, analytics and so on, as well as regular components such as presentation and database.

We'll explore three different designs here – traditional monolithic design, monolithic design with services and μServices design.

The following diagram explains the traditional monolithic application design. This design was widely used before SOA became popular:

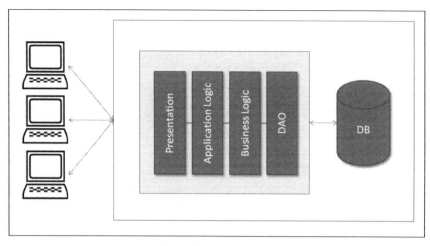

Traditional monolithic design

In traditional monolithic design, everything is bundled in the same archive such as presentation code, application logic and business logic code, and DAO and related code that interacts with the database files or another source.

After SOA, applications started being developed based on services, where each component provides the services to other components or external entities. The following diagram depicts the monolithic application with different services; here services are being used with a presentation component. All services, the presentation component, or any other components are bundled together:

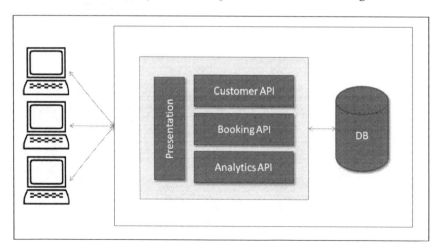

Monolithic design with services

The following third design depicts the µServices. Here, each component represents autonomy. Each component could be developed, built, tested, and deployed independently. Here, even the application UI component could also be a client and consume the µServices. For the purpose of our example, the layer designed is used within µService.

The API gateway provides the interface where different clients can access the individual services and solve the following problems:

- What to do when you want to send different responses to different clients for the same service. For example, a booking service could send different responses to a mobile client (minimal information) and a desktop client (detailed information) providing different details and something different again to a third-party client.

- A response may require fetching information from two or more services:

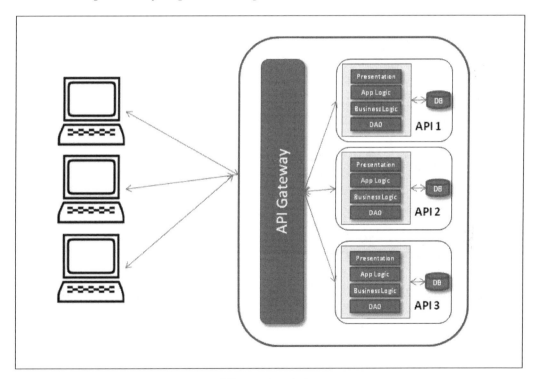

Microservices design

After observing all the sample design diagrams, which are very high-level designs, you might find out that in monolithic design, the components are bundled together and tightly coupled.

All the services are part of the same bundle. Similarly, in the second design figure, you can see a variant of the first figure where all services could have their own layers and form different APIs, but, as shown in the figure, these are also all bundled together.

Conversely, in μServices, design components are not bundles together and have loose coupling. Each service has its own layers and DB and is bundled in a separate archive. All these deployed services provide their specific API such as Customers, Bookings, or Customer. These APIs are ready to consume. Even the UI is also deployed separately and designed using μService. For this reason, it provides various advantages over its monolithic counterpart. I would still remind you that there are some exceptional cases where monolithic app development is highly successful, like Etsy, and peer-to-peer e-commerce web applications.

One dimension scalability

Monolithic applications, which are large when scaled, scale everything as all the components are bundled together. For example, in the case of a restaurant table reservation application, even if you would like to scale the table-booking service, it would scale the whole application; it cannot scale the table-booking service separately. It does not utilize the resource optimally.

In addition, this scaling is one-dimensional. Running more copies of the application provides scale with increasing transaction volume. An operation team could adjust the number of application copies that were using a load-balancer based on the load in a server farm or a cloud. Each of these copies would access the same data source, therefore increasing the memory consumption, and the resulting I/O operations make caching less effective.

μServices gives the flexibility to scale only those services where scale is required and it allows optimal utilization of the resources. As we mentioned previously, when it is needed, you can scale just the table-booking service without affecting any of the other components. It also allows two-dimensional scaling; here we can not only increase the transaction volume but also the data volume using caching (Platform scale).

A development team can then focus on the delivery and shipping of new features, instead of worrying about the scaling issues (Product scale).

μServices could help you scale platform, people, and product dimensions as we have seen previously. People scaling here refers to an increase or decrease in team size depending on μServices' specific development and focus needs.

µService development using RESTful web service development makes it scalable in the sense that the server-end of REST is stateless; this means that there is not much communication between servers, which makes it horizontally scalable.

Release rollback in case of failure

Since, monolithic applications are either bundled in the same archive or contained in a single directory, they prevent the deployment of code modularity. For example, many of you may have experienced the pain of delaying rolling out the whole release due to the failure of one feature.

To resolve these situations, µServices gives us flexibility to rollback only those features that have failed. It's a very flexible and productive approach. For example, let's assume you are the member of an online shopping portal development team and want to develop an app based on µServices. You can divide your app based on different domains such as products, payments, cart and so on, and package all these components as separate packages. Once you have deployed all these packages separately, these would act as single components that can be developed, tested and deployed independently, and called µService.

Now, let's see how that helps you. Let's say that after a production release launching new features, enhancements, and bug fixes, you find flaws in the payment service that need an immediate fix. Since the architecture you have used is based on µServices, you can rollback the payment service instead of rolling back the whole release, if your application architecture allows, or apply the fixes to the µServics payment service without affecting the other services. This not only allows you to handle failure properly, but also helps to deliver the features/fixes swiftly to customer.

Problems in adopting new technologies

Monolithic applications are mostly developed and enhanced based on the technologies primarily used during the initial development of a project or a product. It makes it very difficult to introduce new technology at a later stage of the development or once the product is in a mature state (for example, after a few years). In addition, different modules in the same project that depend on different versions of the same library make this more challenging.

Technology is improving year on year. For example, your system might be designed in Java and then, a few years later, you want to develop a new service in Ruby on rails or NodeJS because of a business need or to utilize the advantages of new technologies. It would be very difficult to utilize the new technology in an existing monolithic application.

It is not just about code-level integration but also about testing and deployment. It is possible to adopt a new technology by re-writing the entire application, but it is time consuming and a risky thing to do.

On the other hand, because of its component-based development and design, µServices gives us the flexibility to use any technology, new or old, for its development. It does not restrict you to using specific technologies, it gives a new paradigm to your development and engineering activities. You can use Ruby on Rails, NodeJS or any other technology at any time.

So, how is it achieved? Well, it's very simple. µServices-based application code does not bundle into a single archive and is not stored in a single directory. Each µService has its own archive and is deployed separately. A new service could be developed in an isolated environment and could be tested and deployed without any technology issues. As you know, µServices also owns its own separate processes; it serves its purpose without any conflict such as shared resources with tight coupling, and processes remain independent.

Since a µService is by definition a small, self-contained function, it provides a low-risk opportunity to try a new technology. That is definitely not the case where monolithic systems are concerned.

You can also make your Microservice available as open source software so it can be used by others, and if required it may interoperate with a closed source proprietary one, which is not possible with monolithic applications.

Alignment with Agile practices

There is no question that monolithic applications can be developed using agile practices and these are being developed. **Continuous Integration** (CI) and **Continuous Deployment** (CD) could be used, but, the question is – does it use agile practices effectively? Let's examine the following points:

- For example, when there is a high probability of having stories dependent on each other, and there could be various scenarios, a story could not be taken up until the dependent story is not complete
- The build takes more time as the code size increases
- The frequent deployment of a large monolithic application is a difficult task to achieve
- You would have to redeploy the whole application even if you updated a single component

- Redeployment may cause problems to already running components, for example a job scheduler may change whether components impact it or not

- The risk of redeployment may increase if a single changed component does not work properly or if it needs more fixes

- UI developers always need more redeployment, which is quite risky and time-consuming for large monolithic applications

The preceding issues can be tackled very easily by μServices, for example, UI developers may have their own UI component that can be developed, built, tested, and deployed separately. Similarly, other μServices might also be deployable independently and because of their autonomous characteristics, the risk of system failure is reduced. Another advantage for development purposes is that UI developers can make use of the JSON object and mock Ajax calls to develop the UI, which can be taken up in an isolated manner. After development completes, developers can consume the actual APIs and test the functionality. To summarize, you could say that μServices development is swift and it aligns well with the incremental needs of businesses.

Ease of development – could be done better

Generally, large monolithic application code is the toughest to understand for developers, and it takes time before a new developer can become productive. Even loading the large monolithic application into IDE is troublesome, and it makes IDE slower and the developer less productive.

A change in a large monolithic application is difficult to implement and takes more time due to a large code base, and there will be a high risk of bugs if impact analysis is not done properly and thoroughly. Therefore, it becomes a prerequisite for developers to do thorough impact analysis before implementing changes.

In monolithic applications, dependencies build up over time as all components bundled together. Therefore, risk associated with code change rises exponentially as code changes (number of modified lines of code) grows.

When a code base is huge and more than 100 developers are working on it, it becomes very difficult to build products and implement new features because of the previously mentioned reason. You need to make sure that everything is in place, and that everything is coordinated. A well-designed and documented API helps a lot in such cases.

Netflix, the on-demand Internet streaming provider, had problems getting their application developed with around 100 people. Then, they used a cloud and broke up the app into separate pieces. These ended up being microservices. Microservices grew from the desire for speed and agility and to deploy teams independently.

Micro-components are made loosely coupled thanks to their exposed API, which can be continuously integration tested. With μServices' continuous release cycle, changes are small and developers can rapidly exploit them with a regression test, then go over them and fix the eventual defects found, reducing the risk of a deployment. This results in higher velocity with a lower associated risk.

Owing to the separation of functionality and single responsibility principle, μServices makes teams very productive. You can find a number of examples online where large projects have been developed with minimum team sizes such as eight to ten developers.

Developers can have better focus with smaller code and resultant better feature implementation that leads to a higher empathic relationship with the users of the product. This conduces better motivation and clarity in feature implementation. Empathic relationship with the users allows a shorter feedback loop, and better and speedy prioritization of the feature pipeline. Shorter feedback loop makes defects detection also faster.

Each μServices team works independently and new features or ideas can be implemented without being coordinated with larger audiences. The implementation of end-point failures handling is also easily achieved in the μServices design.

Recently, at one of the conferences, a team demonstrated how they had developed a μServices-based transport-tracking application including iOS and Android apps within 10 weeks, which had Uber-type tracking features. A big consulting firm gave a seven months estimation for the same app to his client. It shows how μServices is aligned with agile methodologies and CI/CD.

Microservices build pipeline

Microservices could also be built and tested using the popular CI/CD tools such as Jenkins, TeamCity, and so on. It is very similar to how a build is done in a monolithic application. In microservices, each microservice is treated like a small application.

For example, once you commit the code in the repository (SCM), CI/CD tools triggers the build process:

- Cleaning code
- Code compilation

- Unit test execution
- Building the application archives
- Deployment on various servers such as Dev, QA, and so on
- Functional and integration test execution
- Creating image containers
- Any other steps

Then, release-build triggers that change the SNAPSHOT or RELEASE version in `pom.xml` (in case of Maven) build the artifacts as described in the normal build trigger. Publish the artifacts to the `artifacts` repository. Tag this version in the repository. If you use the container image then build the container image.

Deployment using a container such as Docker

Owing to the design of µServices, you need to have an environment that provides flexibility, agility and smoothness for continuous integration and deployment as well as for shipment. µServices deployments need speed, isolation management and an agile life cycle.

Products and software can also be shipped using the concept of an intermodal-container model. An intermodal-container is a large standardized container, designed for intermodal freight transport. It allows cargo to use different modes of transport – truck, rail, or ship without unloading and reloading. This is an efficient and secure way of storing and transporting stuff. It resolves the problem of shipping, which previously had been a time consuming, labor-intensive process, and repeated handling often broke fragile goods.

Shipping containers encapsulate their content. Similarly, software containers are starting to be used to encapsulate their contents (products, apps, dependencies, and so on).

Previously, **virtual machines (VMs)** were used to create software images that could be deployed where needed. Later, containers such as Docker became more popular as they were compatible with both traditional virtual stations systems and cloud environments. For example, it is not practical to deploy more than a couple of VMs on a developer's laptop. Building and booting a VM machine is usually I/O intensive and consequently slow.

Containers

A container (for example, Linux containers) provides a lightweight runtime environment consisting of the core features of virtual machines and the isolated services of operating systems. This makes the packaging and execution of μServices easy and smooth.

As the following diagram shows, a container runs as an application (μService) within the operating system. The OS sits on top of the hardware and each OS could have multiple containers, with a container running the application.

A container makes use of an operating system's kernel interfaces such as cnames and namespaces that allow multiple containers to share the same kernel while running in complete isolation to one another. This gives the advantage of not having to complete an OS installation for each usage; the result being that it removes the overhead. It also makes optimal use of the hardware.

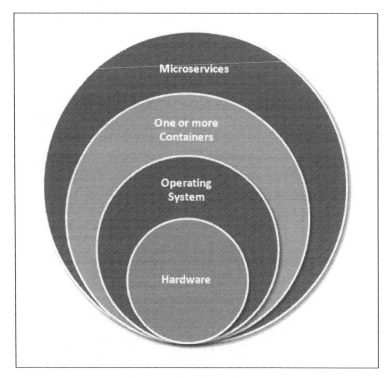

Layer diagram for containers

Docker

Container technology is one of the fastest growing technologies today and Docker leads this segment. Docker is an open source project and was launched in 2013. Ten thousand developers tried it after its interactive tutorial launched in August 2013. It was downloaded 2.75 million times by the time of the launch of its 1.0 release in June 2013. Many large companies have signed the partnership agreement with Docker such as Microsoft, Red Hat, HP, OpenStack and service providers such as Amazon web services, IBM, and Google.

As we mentioned earlier, Docker also makes use of the Linux kernel features, such as cgroups and namespaces to ensure resource isolation and packaging of the application with its dependencies. This packaging of dependencies enables an application to run as expected across different Linux operating systems/distributions; supporting a level of portability. Furthermore this portability allows developers to develop an application in any language and then easily deploy it from a laptop to a test or production server.

 Docker runs natively on Linux. However, you can also run Docker on Windows and Mac OS using VirtualBox and boot2docker.

Containers are comprised of just the application and its dependencies including the basic operating system. This makes it lightweight and efficient in terms of resource utilization.. Developers and system administrators get interested in container's portability and efficient resource utilization.

Everything in a Docker container executes natively on the host and uses the host kernel directly. Each container has its own user namespace.

Docker's architecture

As specified on Docker documentation, Docker architecture uses client-server architecture. As shown in the following figure (sourced from Docker's website), the Docker client is primary a user interface that is used by an end user; clients communicate back and forth with a Docker daemon. The Docker daemon does the heavy lifting of building, running, and distributing your Docker containers. The Docker client and the daemon can run on the same system, or different machines. The Docker client and daemon communicate via sockets or through a RESTful API. Docker registers are public or private Docker image repositories from which you upload or download images, for example Docker Hub (hub.docker.com) is a public Docker registry.

The primary components of Docker are a Docker image and a Docker container.

Docker image

A Docker image is a read-only template. For example, an image could contain an Ubuntu operating system with Apache web server and your web application installed. Docker images are a build component of Docker. Images are used to create Docker containers. Dockers provide a simple way to build new images or update existing images. You can also use images created by others.

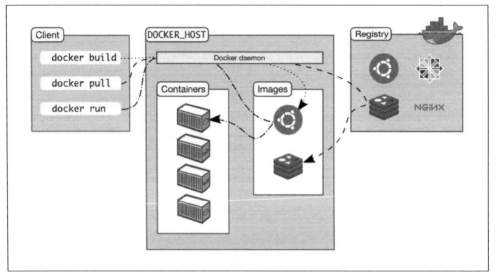

Docker's architecture

Docker container

A Docker container is created from a Docker image. Docker works so that the container can only see its own processes, and have its own filesystem layered onto a host filesystem and a networking stack, which pipes to the host-networking stack. Docker containers can be run, started, stopped, moved or deleted.

Deployment

µServices deployment with Docker deals with three parts:

1. Application packaging, for example, `jar`
2. Building Docker image with `jar` and dependencies using a Docker instruction file, the Dockerfile and command `docker build`. It helps to repeatedly create the image.
3. Docker container execution from this newly built image using command `docker run`.

The preceding information will help you to understand the basics of Docker. You will learn more about Docker and its practical usage in *Chapter 5, Deployment and Testing*. Source and reference: `https://docs.docker.com`.

Summary

In this chapter, you have learned or rehearsed the high-level design of large software projects from traditional monolithic to µServices applications. You were also introduced to a brief history of µServices, the limitation of monolithic applications, and the benefits and flexibility that microservices offers. I hope this chapter helped you to understand the common problems faced in a production environment by monolithic applications and how microservices can resolve such problem. You were also introduced to lightweight and efficient Docker containers, and saw how containerization is an excellent way to simplify microservices deployment.

In the next chapter, you will get to know about setting up the development environment from IDE, and other development tools, to different libraries We will deal with creating basic projects and setting up Spring Boot configuration to build and develop our first microservice. Here, we will use Java 8 as the language and Spring Boot for our project.

2
Setting Up the Development Environment

This chapter focuses on the development environment setup and configurations. If you are familiar with the tools and libraries, you could skip this chapter and continue with *Chapter 3, Domain-Driven Design* where you could explore the domain driven design.

This chapter will cover the following topics:

- Spring Boot configuration
- Sample REST program
- Build setup
- REST API testing using the Postman Chrome extension
- NetBeans – installation and setup

This book will use only the open source tools and frameworks for examples and code. The book will also use Java 8 as its programming language, and the application framework will be based on the Spring framework. This book makes use of Spring Boot to develop microservices.

NetBeans Integrated Development Environment (IDE) that provides state of the art support for both Java and JavaScript, is sufficient for our needs. It has evolved a lot over the years and has built-in support for most of the technologies used by this book, such as Maven, Spring Boot and so on. Therefore, I would recommend you to use NetBeans IDE. You are, however free to use any IDE.

We will use Spring Boot to develop the REST services and microservices. Opting for the most popular of Spring frameworks, Spring Boot, or its subset Spring Cloud in this book was a conscious decision. Because of this, we don't need to write applications from scratch and it provides default configuration for most of the stuff for Cloud applications. A Spring Boot overview is provided in Spring Boot's configuration section. If you are new to Spring Boot, this would definitely help you.

We will use Maven as our build tool. As with the IDE, you can use whichever build tool you want, for example Gradle or Ant. We will use the embedded Jetty as our web server but another alternative is to use an embedded Tomcat web server. We will also use the Postman extension of Chrome for testing our REST services.

We will start with Spring Boot Configurations. If you are new to NetBeans or are facing issues in setting up the environment, you can refer to the NetBeans IDE installation section explained in the last section; otherwise you can skip that section altogether.

Spring Boot configuration

Spring Boot is an obvious choice to develop state of the art production-ready applications specific to Spring. Its website also states its real advantages:

> *"Takes an opinionated view of building production-ready Spring applications. Spring Boot favors convention over configuration and is designed to get you up and running as quickly as possible."*

Spring Boot overview

Spring Boot is an amazing Spring tool created by Pivotal and released in April 2014 (GA). It was developed based on request of SPR-9888 (`https://jira.spring.io/browse/SPR-9888`) with the title *Improved support for 'containerless' web application architectures.*

You must be wondering why containerless? Because, today's cloud environment or PaaS provides most of the features offered by container-based web architectures such as reliability, management or scaling. Therefore, Spring Boot focuses on making itself an ultra light container.

Spring Boot is preconfigured to make production-ready web applications very easily. Spring Initializer (`http://start.spring.io`) is a page where you can select build tools such as Maven or Gradle, project metadata such as group, artifact and dependencies. Once, you feed the required fields you can just click on the **Generate Project** button, which will give you the Spring Boot project that you can use for your production application.

On this page, the default packaging option is `jar`. We'll also use jar packaging for our microservices development. The reason is very simple: it makes microservices development easier. Just think how difficult it would be to manage and create an infrastructure where each microservice runs on its own server instance.

Josh Long shared in his talk in one of the Spring IOs:

> *"It is better to make Jar, not War."*

Later, we will use the Spring Cloud that is a wrapper on top of Spring Boot.

Adding Spring Boot to the rest sample

At the time of writing the book, Spring Boot 1.2.5 release version was available. You can use the latest released version. Spring Boot uses Spring 4 (4.1.7 release).

Open the `pom.xml` (available under **restsample** | **Project Files**) to add Spring Boot to your rest sample project:

```xml
<?xml version="1.0" encoding="UTF-8"?>
<project xmlns="http://maven.apache.org/POM/4.0.0" xmlns:xsi="http://
www.w3.org/2001/XMLSchema-instance" xsi:schemaLocation="http://maven.
apache.org/POM/4.0.0 http://maven.apache.org/xsd/maven-4.0.0.xsd">
    <modelVersion>4.0.0</modelVersion>
    <groupId>com.packtpub.mmj</groupId>
    <artifactId>restsample</artifactId>
    <version>1.0-SNAPSHOT</version>
    <packaging>jar</packaging>
    <parent>
        <groupId>org.springframework.boot</groupId>
        <artifactId>spring-boot-starter-parent</artifactId>
        <version>1.2.5.RELEASE</version>
    </parent>
```

```
<properties>
    <project.build.sourceEncoding>UTF-8</project.build.
sourceEncoding>
    <spring-boot-version>1.2.5.RELEASE</spring-boot-version>
</properties>
<dependencies>
    <dependency>
        <groupId>org.springframework.boot</groupId>
        <artifactId>spring-boot-starter-web</artifactId>
        <version>${spring-boot-version}</version>
    </dependency>
</dependencies>
</project>
```

If you are adding these dependencies for the first time, you need to download the dependencies by right clicking on the Dependencies folder under **restsample** project in the **Projects** pane shown as follows:

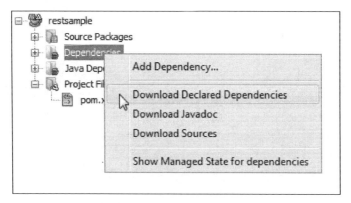

Download Maven Dependencies in NetBeans

Similarly, to resolve the project problems, right-click on the NetBeans project **restsample** and opt for the **Resolve Project Problems....** It will open the dialog shown as follows. Click on the **Resolve...** button to resolve the issues:

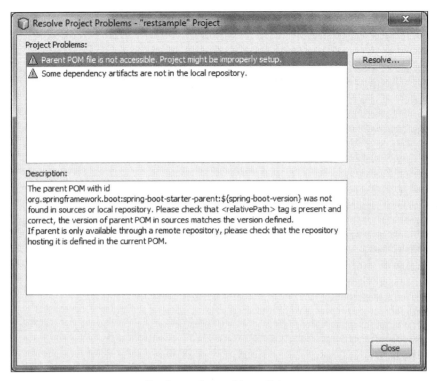

Resolve project problems dialog

 If you are using Maven behind the proxy, then update the proxies settings in `<NetBeans Installation Directory>\java\maven\conf\settings.xml`. You may need to restart the NetBeans IDE

The preceding steps will download all the required dependencies from a remote Maven repository if the declared dependencies and transitive dependencies are not available in a local Maven repository. If you are downloading the dependencies for the first time, then it may take a bit of time, depending on your Internet speed.

Adding a Jetty-embedded server

Spring Boot by default provides Apache Tomcat as an embedded application container. This book will use the Jetty-embedded application container in the place of Apache Tomcat. Therefore, we need to add a Jetty application container dependency to support the Jetty web server.

Jetty also allows you to read keys or trust stores using classpath that is, you don't need to keep these stores outside the JAR files. If you use Tomcat with SSL, then you will need to access the key store or trust store directly from the filesystem but you can't do that using the classpath. The result is that you can't read a key store or a trust store within a JAR file because Tomcat requires that the key store (and trust store if you're using one) is directly accessible on the filesystem.

This limitation doesn't apply to Jetty, which allows the reading of keys or trust stores within a JAR file:

```
<dependencies>
<dependency>
        <groupId>org.springframework.boot</groupId>
            <artifactId>spring-boot-starter-web</artifactId>
            <exclusions>
              <exclusion>
<groupId>org.springframework.boot</groupId>
<artifactId>spring-boot-starter-tomcat</artifactId>
                </exclusion>
            </exclusions>
</dependency>
<dependency>
<groupId>org.springframework.boot</groupId>
<artifactId>spring-boot-starter-jetty</artifactId>
</dependency>
</dependencies>
```

Sample REST program

You will use a simple approach to building a stand-alone application. It packages everything into a single, executable JAR file, driven by a `main()` method. Along the way, you use Spring's support for embedding the Jetty servlet container as the HTTP runtime, instead of deploying it to an external instance. Therefore, we would create the executable JAR in place of the war that needs to be deployed on external web servers.

Now, as you are ready with Spring Boot in NetBeans IDE, you could create your sample web service. You will create a Math API that performs simple calculations and generates the result as JSON.

Let's discuss how we can call and get responses from REST services.

The service will handle GET requests for /calculation/sqrt or /calculation/power and so on. The GET request should return a 200 OK response with JSON in the body that represents the square root of given number. It should look something like this:

```
{
  "function": "sqrt",
  "input": [
    "144"
  ],
  "output": [
    "12.0"
  ]
}
```

The input field is the input parameter for the square root function, and the content is the textual representation of the result.

You could create a resource representation class to model the representation by using **Plain Old Java Object (POJO)** with fields, constructors, setters, and getters for the input, output, and function data:

```java
package com.packtpub.mmj.restsample.model;

import java.util.List;

public class Calculation {

    String function;
    private List<String> input;
    private List<String> output;

    public Calculation(List<String> input, List<String> output, String function) {
        this.function = function;
        this.input = input;
        this.output = output;
    }

    public List<String> getInput() {
        return input;
    }

    public void setInput(List<String> input) {
        this.input = input;
    }
```

```
public List<String> getOutput() {
    return output;
}

public void setOutput(List<String> output) {
    this.output = output;
}

public String getFunction() {
    return function;
}

public void setFunction(String function) {
    this.function = function;
}

}
```

Writing the REST controller class

Roy Fielding defined and introduced the term **REST, Representational State Transfer** in his doctoral dissertation. REST is a style of software architecture for a distributed hypermedia system such as WWW. RESTful refers to those systems that conform to REST architecture properties, principles, and constraints.

Now, you'll create a REST controller to handle the calculation resource. The controller handles the HTTP requests in the Spring RESTful web service implementation.

@RestController

@RestController is a class-level annotation used for the resource class introduced in Spring 4. It is a combination of @Controller and @ResponseBody, and because of it, class returns a domain object instead of a view.

In the following code, you can see that the CalculationController class handles GET requests for /calculation by returning a new instance of the calculation class.

We will implement two URLs for a calculation resource – the square root (Math. sqrt() function) as /calculations/sqrt URL, and power (Math.pow() function) as /calculation/power URL.

@RequestMapping

`@RequestMapping` annotation is used at class-level to map the `/calculation`
URI to `CalculationController` class that is, it ensures that the HTTP request to
`/calculation` is mapped to the `CalculationController` class. Based on the path
defined using the annotation `@RequestMapping` of the URI (postfix of `/calculation`,
for example, `/calculation/sqrt/144`), it would be mapped to respective methods.
Here, the request mapping `/calculation/sqrt` is mapped to the `sqrt()` method
and `/calculation/power` is mapped to the `pow()` method.

You might have also observed that we have not defined what request method (GET/
POST/PUT, and so on) these methods would use. The `@RequestMapping` annotation
maps all the HTTP request methods by default. You could use specific methods
by using the method property of `RequestMapping`. For example, you could write
a `@RequestMethod` annotation in the following way to use the POST method:

```
@RequestMapping(value = "/power", method = POST)
```

For passing the parameters along the way, the sample demonstrates both request
parameters and path parameters using annotations `@RequestParam` and `@
PathVariable` respectively.

@RequestParam

`@RequestParam` is responsible for binding the query parameter to the parameter
of the controller's method. For example, the QueryParam base and exponent
are bound to parameters `b` and `e` of method `pow()` of `CalculationController`
respectively. Both of the query parameters of the `pow()` method are required since
we are not using any default value for them. Default values for query parameters
could be set using the `defaultValue` property of `@RequestParam` for example
`@RequestParam(value="base", defaultValue="2")`, here, if the user does not
pass the query parameter base, then the default value 2 would be used for the base.

If no `defaultValue` is defined, and the user doesn't provide the request parameter,
then `RestController` returns the HTTP status code 400 with the message **400
Required String parameter base is not present**. It always uses the reference of the
first required parameter if more than one of the request parameters is missing:

```
{
   "timestamp": 1464678493402,
   "status": 400,
   "error": "Bad Request",
   "exception": "org.springframework.web.bind.
MissingServletRequestParameterException",
```

```
        "message": "Required String parameter 'base' is not present",
        "path": "/calculation/power/"
}
```

@PathVariable

`@PathVariable` helps you to create the dynamic URIs. `@PathVariable` annotation allows you to map Java parameters to a path parameter. It works with `@RequestMapping` where placeholder is created in URI then the same placeholder name is used either as a `PathVariable` or a method parameter, as you can see in the `CalculationController` class's method `sqrt()`. Here, the value placeholder is created inside the `@RequestMapping` and the same value is assigned to the value of the `@PathVariable`.

Method `sqrt()` takes the parameter in the URI in place of the request parameter. For example, `http://localhost:8080/calculation/sqrt/144`. Here, the `144` value is passed as the path parameter and this URL should return the square root of 144 that is, `12`.

To use the basic check in place, we use the regular expression `"^-?+\\d+\\.?+\\d*$"` to allow only valid numbers in parameters. If non-numeric values are passed, the respective method adds an error message in the output key of the JSON.

> `CalculationController` also uses the regular expression `.+` in the `path` variable (path parameter) to allow the decimal point(`.`) in numeric values - `/path/{variable:.+}`. Spring ignores anything after the last dot. Spring default behavior takes it as a file extension.
>
> There are other alternatives such as adding a slash at the end (`/path/{variable}/`) or overriding the method `configurePathMatch()` of `WebMvcConfigurerAdapter` by setting the `useRegisteredSuffixPatternMatch` to true, using `PathMatchConfigurer` (available in Spring 4.0.1+).

```
package com.packtpub.mmj.restsample.resources;

package com.packtpub.mmj.restsample.resources;

import com.packtpub.mmj.restsample.model.Calculation;
import java.util.ArrayList;
import java.util.List;
import org.springframework.web.bind.annotation.PathVariable;
import org.springframework.web.bind.annotation.RequestMapping;
```

```
import static org.springframework.web.bind.annotation.RequestMethod.
GET;
import org.springframework.web.bind.annotation.RequestParam;
import org.springframework.web.bind.annotation.RestController;

@RestController
@RequestMapping("/calculation")
public class CalculationController {

    private static final String PATTERN = "^-?+\\d+\\.?+\\d*$";

    @RequestMapping("/power")
    public Calculation pow(@RequestParam(value = "base") String b, @
RequestParam(value = "exponent") String e) {
        List<String> input = new ArrayList();
        input.add(b);
        input.add(e);
        List<String> output = new ArrayList();
        String powValue = "";
        if (b != null && e != null && b.matches(PATTERN) &&
e.matches(PATTERN)) {
            powValue = String.valueOf(Math.pow(Double.valueOf(b),
Double.valueOf(e)));
        } else {
            powValue = "Base or/and Exponent is/are not set to numeric
value.";
        }
        output.add(powValue);
        return new Calculation(input, output, "power");
    }

    @RequestMapping(value = "/sqrt/{value:.+}", method = GET)
    public Calculation sqrt(@PathVariable(value = "value") String
aValue) {
        List<String> input = new ArrayList();
        input.add(aValue);
        List<String> output = new ArrayList();
        String sqrtValue = "";
        if (aValue != null && aValue.matches(PATTERN)) {
            sqrtValue = String.valueOf(Math.sqrt(Double.
valueOf(aValue)));
        } else {
            sqrtValue = "Input value is not set to numeric value.";
        }
```

```
                output.add(sqrtValue);
                return new Calculation(input, output, "sqrt");
        }
}
```

Here, we are exposing only the `power` and `sqrt` functions for the `Calculation` resource using URI `/calculation/power` and `/calculation/sqrt`.

 Here, we are using sqrt and power as a part of the URI, which we have used for demonstration purposes only. Ideally, these should have been passed as value of a request parameter "function"; or something similar based on endpoint design formation.

One interesting thing here is that due to Spring's HTTP message converter support, the `Calculation` object gets converted to JSON automatically. You don't need to do this conversion manually. If Jackson 2 is on the classpath, Spring's `MappingJackson2HttpMessageConverter` converts the `Calculation` object to JSON.

Making a sample REST app executable

Create a class `RestSampleApp` with the annotation `SpringBootApplication`. The `main()` method uses Spring Boot's `SpringApplication.run()` method to launch an application.

We will annotate the `RestSampleApp` class with the `@SpringBootApplication` that adds all of the following tags implicitly:

- The `@Configuration` annotation tags the class as a source of Bean definitions for the application context.

- The `@EnableAutoConfiguration` annotation indicates that Spring Boot is to start adding beans based on classpath settings, other beans, and various property settings.

- The `@EnableWebMvc` annotation is added if Spring Boot finds the spring-webmvc on the classpath. It treats the application as a web application and activates key behaviors such as setting up a DispatcherServlet.

- The `@ComponentScan` annotation tells Spring to look for other components, configurations, and services in the given package:

```
package com.packtpub.mmj.restsample;

import org.springframework.boot.SpringApplication;
import org.springframework.boot.autoconfigure.
SpringBootApplication;

@SpringBootApplication
public class RestSampleApp {

    public static void main(String[] args) {
        SpringApplication.run(RestSampleApp.class, args);
    }
}
```

This web application is 100 percent pure Java and you didn't have to deal with configuring any plumbing or infrastructure using XML; instead it uses the Java annotation, that is made even simpler by Spring Boot. Therefore, there wasn't a single line of XML except `pom.xml` for Maven. There wasn't even a `web.xml` file.

Setting up the application build

Whatever `pom.xml` we have used until now is enough to execute our sample REST service. This service would package the code into a JAR. To make this JAR executable we need to opt for the following options:

Running the Maven tool

Here, we use the Maven tool to execute the generated JAR, steps for the same are as follows:

1. Right-click on the `pom.xml`.
2. Select **run-maven | Goals...** from the pop-up menu. It will open the dialog. Type `spring-boot:run` in the **Goals** field. We have used the released version of Spring Boot in the code. However, if you are using the snapshot release, you can check the **Update Snapshots** checkbox. To use it in the future, type `spring-boot-run` in the **Remember as** field.

3. Next time, you could directly click **run-maven | Goals | spring-boot-run** to execute the project:

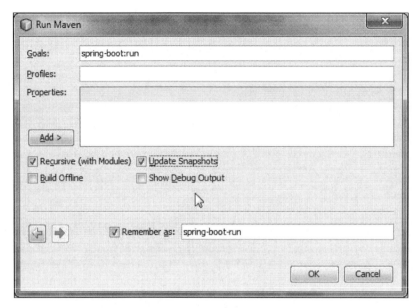

Run Maven dialog

4. Click on **OK** to execute the project.

Executing with the Java command

To build the JAR, perform the `mvn clean` package Maven goal. It creates the JAR file in a `target` directory, then, the JAR can be executed using the command:

```
java -jar target/restsample-1.0-SNAPSHOT.jar
```

REST API testing using the Postman Chrome extension

This book uses the Postman – REST Client extension for Chrome to test our REST service. We use the 0.8.4.16 version that can be downloaded using `https://chrome.google.com/webstore/detail/postman-rest-client/fdmmgilgnpjigdojojpjoooidkmcomcm`. This extension is no longer searchable but you can add it to your Chrome using the given link. You can also use the Postman Chrome app or any other REST Client to test your sample REST application:

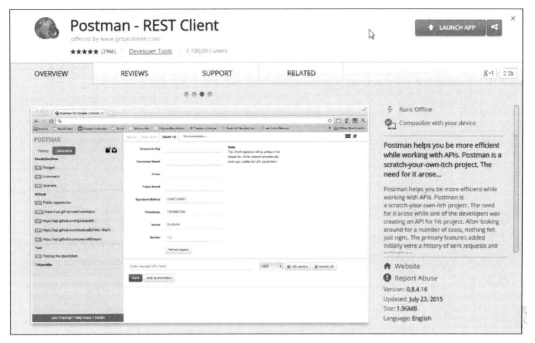

Postman – Rest Client Chrome extension

Let's test our first REST resource once you have the Postman – REST Client installed. We start the Postman – REST Client from either the start menu or from a shortcut.

 By default the embedded web server starts on port 8080. Therefore, we need to use the `http://localhost:8080/<resource>` URL for accessing the sample REST application. Example: `http://localhost:8080/calculation/sqrt/144`.

Once it's started, you can type the Calculation REST URL for `sqrt` and value `144` as the path parameter. You could see it in the following image. This URL is entered in the URL (Enter request URL here) input field of the Postman extension. By default, the request method is GET. We use the default value for the request method, as we have also written our RESTful service to serve the request GET method.

Once you are ready with your input data as mentioned above, you can submit the request by clicking the **Send** button. You can see in the following image that the response code `200` is returned by your sample rest service. You can find the **Status** label in the following image to see the **200 OK** code. A successful request also returns the JSON data of the Calculation Resource, shown in the `Pretty` tab in the screenshot. The returned JSON shows the `sqrt`, value of the function key. It also displays `144` and `12.0` as the input and output lists respectively:

Calculation (sqrt) resource test with Postman

Similarly, we also test our sample REST service for the calculating `power` function. We input the following data in the Postman extension:

- **URL:** `http://localhost:8080/calculation/power?base=2&exponent=4`
- **Request method:** `GET`

Here, we are passing the request parameters base and exponent with values of 2 and 4 respectively. It returns the following JSON with a response status of **200** as shown in the following screenshot.

Returned JSON:

```
{
    "function": "power",
    "input": [
        "2",
        "4"
    ],
    "output": [
        "16.0"
    ]
}
```

Calculation (power) resource test with Postman

Some more positive test scenarios

In the following table, all the URLs start with `http://localhost:8080`:

URL	Output JSON
`/calculation/sqrt/12344.234`	```{ "function": "sqrt", "input": ["12344.234"], "output": ["111.1046083652699"] }```
`/calculation/sqrt/-9344.34` `Math.sqrt` function's special scenario: • If the argument is NaN or less than zero, then the result is NaN	```{ "function": "sqrt", "input": ["-9344.34"], "output": ["NaN"] }```
`/calculation/` `power?base=2.09&exponent=4.5`	```{ "function": "power", "input": ["2.09", "4.5"], "output": ["27.58406626826615"] }```

URL	Output JSON
`/calculation/power?base=-92.9&exponent=-4`	```json { "function": "power", "input": ["-92.9", "-4"], "output": ["1.3425706351762353E-8"] } ```

Negative test scenarios

Similarly, you could also perform some negative scenarios as shown in the following table. In this table, all the URLs start with `http://localhost:8080`:

URL	Output JSON
`/calculation/power?base=2a&exponent=4`	```json { "function": "power", "input": ["2a", "4"], "output": ["Base or/and Exponent is/are not set to numeric value."] } ```
`/calculation/power?base=2&exponent=4b`	```json { "function": "power", "input": ["2", "4b"], "output": ["Base or/and Exponent is/are not set to numeric value."] } ```

URL	Output JSON

`/calculation/`
`power?base=2.0a&exponent=a4`
	`{`
	    `"function": "power",`
	    `"input": [`
	        `"2.0a",`
	        `"a4"`
	    `],`
	    `"output": [`
	        `"Base or/and`
	`Exponent is/are not set`
	`to numeric value."`
	        `]`
	`}`

`/calculation/sqrt/144a`	`{`
	    `"function": "sqrt",`
	    `"input": [`
	        `"144a"`
	    `],`
	    `"output": [`
	        `"Input value`
	`is not set to numeric`
	`value."`
	        `]`
	`}`

`/calculation/sqrt/144.33$`	`{`
	    `"function": "sqrt",`
	    `"input": [`
	        `"144.33$"`
	    `],`
	    `"output": [`
	        `"Input value`
	`is not set to numeric`
	`value."`
	        `]`
	`}`

NetBeans IDE installation and setup

NetBeans IDE is free and open source, and has a big community of users. You can download the NetBeans IDE from `https://netbeans.org/downloads/`, its official website.

At the time of writing this book, version 8.0.2 was the latest available version. As shown in the following screenshot, please download all the supported NetBeans bundles, as we'll use Javascript also:

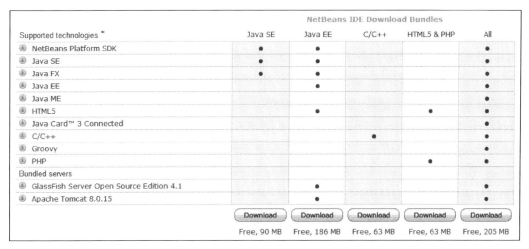

	NetBeans IDE Download Bundles				
Supported technologies *	Java SE	Java EE	C/C++	HTML5 & PHP	All
NetBeans Platform SDK	•	•			•
Java SE	•	•			•
Java FX	•	•			•
Java EE		•			•
Java ME					•
HTML5		•		•	•
Java Card™ 3 Connected					•
C/C++			•		•
Groovy					•
PHP				•	•
Bundled servers					
GlassFish Server Open Source Edition 4.1		•			•
Apache Tomcat 8.0.15		•			
	Download	Download	Download	Download	Download
	Free, 90 MB	Free, 186 MB	Free, 63 MB	Free, 63 MB	Free, 205 MB

NetBeans bundles

After downloading the the installation, execute the installer file. Accept the license agreement as shown in the following screenshot, and follow the rest of the steps to install the NetBeans IDE. Glassfish Server and Apache Tomcat are optional.

JDK 7 or a later version is required for installing and running the All NetBeans Bundles. You can download a standalone JDK 8 from `http://www.oracle.com/technetwork/java/javase/ downloads/index.html`.

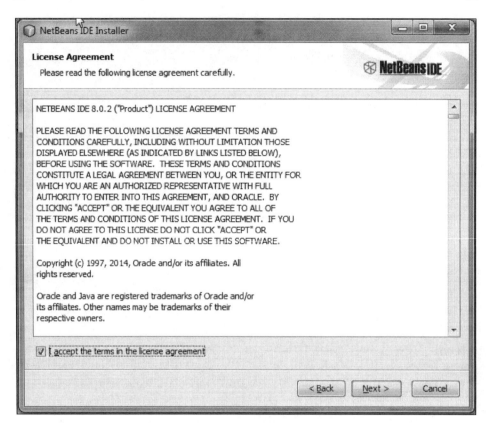

NetBeans Bundles

Once NetBeans the IDE is installed, start the NetBeans IDE. NetBeans IDE should look as follows:

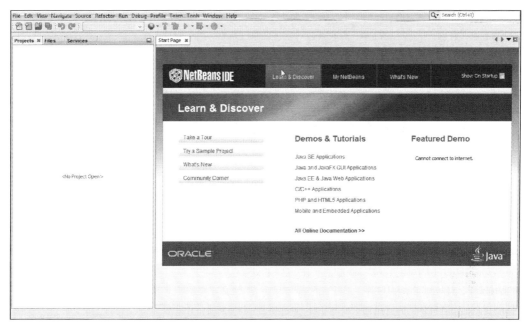

NetBeans start page

Maven and Gradle are both Java build tools. They add dependent libraries to your project, compile your code, set properties, build archives, or do many more related activities. Spring Boot or the Spring Cloud support both Maven and Gradle build tools. However, in this book we'll use the Maven build tool. Please feel free to use Gradle if you prefer.

Maven is already available in NetBeans IDE. Now, we can start a new Maven project to build our first REST app.

Steps for creating a new empty Maven project:

1. Click on **New Project** (*Ctrl + Shift + N*) under the **File** menu. It will open the new project wizard.

2. Select **Maven** in the **Categories** list. Then, select **Java Application** in the **Projects** list (as shown in following screenshot). Then, click on the **Next** button:

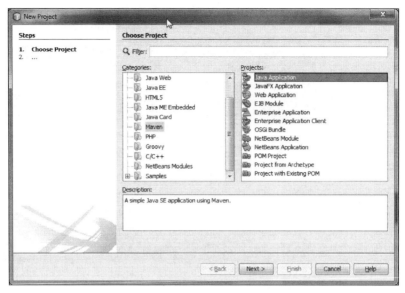

New Project Wizard

3. Now, enter the the project name as restsample. Also, enter the other properties as shown in the following screenshot. Click on **Finish** once all the mandatory fields are entered:

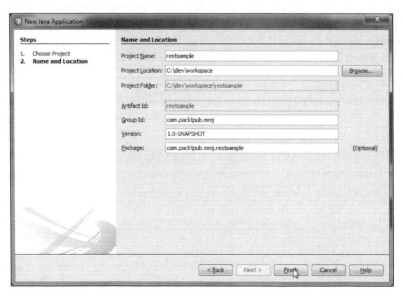

NetBeans Maven project properties

Aggelos Karalias has developed a helpful plugin for NetBeans IDE offering autocomplete support for Spring Boot configuration properties available at `https://github.com/keevosh/nb-springboot-configuration-support`. You can download it from his project page at `http://keevosh.github.io/nb-springboot-configuration-support/`.

You could also use Spring Tool Suite IDE (`https://spring.io/tools`) from Pivotal instead of NetBeans IDE. It's a customized all-in-one Eclipse-based distribution that makes application development easy.

After finishing all the the preceding steps, NetBeans will display a newly created Maven project. You will use this project for creating the sample rest application using Spring Boot.

To use Java 8 as a source, set the **Source/Binary Format** to **1.8** as shown in the following screenshot:

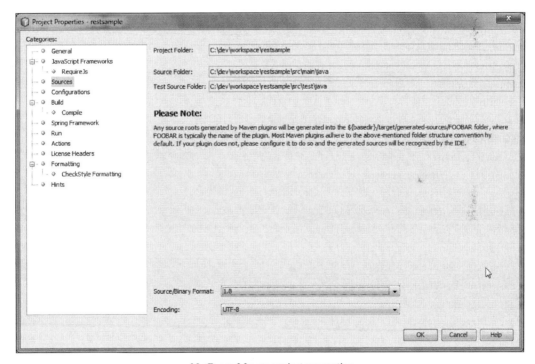

NetBeans Maven project properties

References

- **Spring Boot**: http://projects.spring.io/spring-boot/
- **Download NetBeans**: https://netbeans.org/downloads
- **Representational State Transfer (REST)**: Chapter 5 of Roy Thomas Fielding Ph.D. dissertation "Architectural Styles and the Design of Network-based Software Architectures" - https://www.ics.uci.edu/~fielding/pubs/dissertation/top.htm
- **REST**: https://en.wikipedia.org/wiki/Representational_state_transfer
- **Maven**: https://www.apache.org/
- **Gradle**: http://gradle.org/

Summary

In this chapter, you have explored various aspects of setting up a development environment such as NetBeans IDE setup and installation, Maven configuration, Spring Boot configuration and so on.

You have also learned how to make use of Spring Boot to develop a sample REST service application. We learned how powerful Spring Boot is – it eases development so much that you only have to worry about the actual code, and not about the boilerplate code or configurations that you write. We have also packaged our code into a JAR with an embedded application container Jetty. It allows it to run and access the web application without worrying about the deployment.

In the next chapter, you will learn the **domain-driven design (DDD)** using a sample project that can be used across the rest of the chapters. We'll use the sample project **online table reservation system (OTRS)** to go through various phases of microservices development and understand the DDD. After completing *Chapter 3, Domain-Driven Design* you will learn the fundamentals of DDD. You will understand how to practically use the DDD by design sample services. You will also learn to design the domain models and REST services on top of it.

3
Domain-Driven Design

This chapter sets the tone for rest of the chapters by referring to one sample project. The sample project will be used to explain different microservices concepts from here onwards. This chapter uses this sample project to drive through different combinations of functional and domain services or apps to explain the **domain-driven design (DDD)**. It will help you to learn the fundamentals of DDD and its practical usage. You will also learn the concepts of designing domain models using REST services.

This chapter covers the following topics:

- Fundamentals of DDD
- How to design an application using DDD
- Domain models
- A sample domain model design based on DDD

A good software design is as much the key to the success of a product or services as the functionalities offered by it. It carries equal weight to the success of product; for example, Amazon.com provides the shopping platform but its architecture design makes it different from other similar sites and contributes to its success. It shows how important a software or architecture design is for the success of a product/service. DDD is one of the software design practices and we'll explore it with various theories and practical examples.

DDD is a key design practice that helps to design the microservices of the product that you are developing. Therefore, we'll first explore DDD before jumping into microservices development. DDD uses multilayered architecture as one of its building blocks. After learning this chapter, you will understand the importance of DDD for microservices development.

Domain-driven design fundamentals

An enterprise or cloud application solves business problems and other real world problems. These problems cannot be resolved without knowledge of the domain. For example, you cannot provide a software solution for a financial system such as online stock trading if you don't understand the stock exchanges and their functioning. Therefore, having domain knowledge is a must for solving problems. Now, if you want to offer a solution using software or apps, you need to design it with the help of domain knowledge. When we combine the domain and software design, it offers a software design methodology known as DDD.

When we develop software to implement real world scenarios offering the functionalities of a domain, we create a model of the domain. A model is an abstraction or a blueprint of the domain.

[

Eric Evans coined the term DDD in his book *Domain-Driven Design: Tackling Complexity in the Heart of Software*, published in 2004.
]

Designing this model is not rocket science but it does take a lot of effort, refining and input from domain experts. It is the collective job of software designers, domain experts, and developers. They organize information, divide it into smaller parts, group them logically and create modules. Each module can be taken up individually and can be divided using a similar approach. This process can be followed until we reach the unit level or we cannot divide it any further. A complex project may have more of such iterations and similarly a simple project could have just a single iteration of it.

Once a model is defined and well documented, it can move onto the next stage – code design. So, here we have a software design – a Domain Model and code design – and code implementation of the Domain Model. The Domain Model provides a high level of architecture of a solution (software/app) and the code implementation gives the domain model a life, as a working model.

DDD makes design and development work together. It provides the ability to develop software continuously while keeping the design up to date based on feedback received from the development. It solves one of the limitations offered by Agile and Waterfall methodologies making software maintainable including design and code, as well as keeping app minimum viable.

Design-driven development involves a developer from the initial stage and all meetings where software designers discuss the domain with domain experts in the modeling process. It gives developers the right platform to understand the domain and provides the opportunity to share early feedback of the Domain Model implementation. It removes the bottleneck that appears in later stages when stockholders waits for deliverables.

Building blocks

This section explains the ubiquitous language used and why it is required, the different patterns to be used in model-driven design and the importance of multilayered architecture.

Ubiquitous language

As we have seen, designing a model is the collective effort of software designers, domain experts, and developers and, therefore, it requires a common language to communicate. DDD makes it necessary to use common language and the use of ubiquitous language. Domain models use ubiquitous language in their diagrams, descriptions, presentations, speeches, and meetings. It removes the misunderstanding, misinterpretation and communication gap among them.

Unified Model Language (UML) is widely used and very popular when creating models. It also carries few limitations, for example when you have thousands of classes drawn of a paper, it's difficult to represent class relationships and also understand their abstraction while taking a meaning out of it. Also UML diagrams do not represent the concepts of a model and what objects are supposed to do.

There are other ways to communicate the domain model such as – documents, code, and so on.

Multilayered architecture

Multilayered architecture is a common solution for **DDD**. It contains four layers:

1. Presentation layer or **User Interface (UI)**.
2. Application layer.
3. Domain layer.

4. Infrastructure layer.

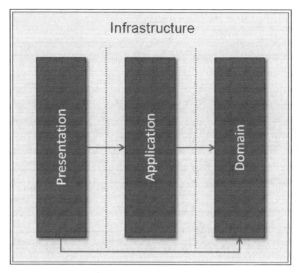

Layered architecture

You can see here that only the domain layer is responsible for the domain model and others are related to other components such as UI, app logic and so on. This layered architecture is very important. It keeps domain-related code separate from other layers.

In this multilayered architecture, each layer contains its respective code and it helps to achieve loose coupling and avoid mixing code from different layers. It also help the product/service's long term maintainability and the ease of enhancements as the change of one layer code does not impact on other components if the change is intended for the respective layer only. Each layer can be switched with another implementation easily with multitier architecture.

Presentation layer

This layer represents the UI and provides the user interface for the interaction and information display. This layer could be a web application, mobile app or a third-party application consuming your services.

Application layer

This layer is responsible for application logic. It maintains and coordinates the overall flow of the product/service. It does not contain business logic or UI. It may hold the state of application objects like tasks in progress. For example, your product REST services would be the part of this application layer.

Domain layer

The domain layer is a very important layer as it contains the domain information and business logic. It holds the state of the business object. It persists the state of the business objects, and communicates these persisted states to the infrastructure layer.

Infrastructure layer

This layer provides support to all the other layers and is responsible for communication among the other layers. It contains the supporting libraries that are used by the other layers. It also implements the persistence of business objects.

To understand the interaction of the different layers, let us take an example of table booking at a restaurant. The end user places a request for a table booking using UI. UI passes the request to the application layer. The application layer fetches the domain objects such as the restaurant, the table with a date and so on from the domain layer. The domain layers fetch these existing persisted objects from the infrastructure and invoke relevant methods to make the booking and persists them back to infrastructure layer. Once, domain objects are persisted, application layer shows the booking confirmation to end user.

Artifacts of domain-driven design

There are different artifacts used in DDD to express, create, and retrieve domain models.

Entities

There are certain categories of objects that are identifiable and remain same throughout the states of the product/services. These objects are NOT defined by its attributes, but by its identity and thread of continuity. These are known as entities.

It sounds pretty simple but carries complexity. You need to understand how we can define the entities. Let's take an example for table booking system, if we have a `restaurant` class with attributes such as restaurant name, address, phone number, establishment data, and so on. We can take two instances of the `restaurant` class that are not identifiable using the restaurant name, as there could be other restaurants with the same name. Similarly, if we go by any other single attributes we will not find any attributes that can singularly identify a unique restaurant. If two restaurants have all the same attribute values, these are the same and are interchangeable with each other. Still, these are not the same entities as both have different references (memory addresses).

Conversely, let's take a class of US citizen. Each citizen has his own social security number. This number is not only unique but remains unchanged throughout the life of the citizen and assures continuity. This citizen object would exist in the memory, would be serialized, and would be removed from the memory and stored in the database. It even exists after the person is dead. It will be kept in the system as long as system exists. A citizen's social security number remains the same irrespective of its representation.

Therefore, creating entities in a product means creating identity. So, now give an identity to any restaurant in the previous example, then either use a combination of attributes such as restaurant name, establishment date and street, or add an identifier such as `restaurant_id` to identify it. This is the basic rule that two identifiers cannot be same. Therefore, when we introduce an identifier for any entity we need to be sure of it.

There are different ways to create a unique identity for objects described as follows:

- Using the primary key in a table.
- Using an automated generated ID by a domain module. A domain program generates the identifier and assigns it to objects that are being persisted among different layers.
- A few real life objects carry user-defined identifiers themselves. For example each country has its own country codes for dialing ISD calls.
- An attribute or combination of attributes can also be used for creating an identifier as explained for the preceding `restaurant` object.

Entities are very important for domain models, therefore, they should be defined from the initial stage of the modeling process. When an object can be identified by its identifier and not by its attributes, a class representing these objects should have a simple definition and care should be taken with the life cycle continuity and identity. It's imperative to say that it is a requirement of identifying objects in this class that have the same attribute values. A defined system should return a unique result for each object if queried. Designers should take care that the model must define what it means to be the same thing.

Value objects

Entities have traits such as, identity, a thread of continuity, and attributes that do not define their identity. **Value objects (VOs)** just have attributes and no conceptual identity. A best practice is to keep value Objects as immutable objects. If possible, you should even keep entity objects immutable too.

Entity concepts may bias you to keep all objects as entities, a uniquely identifiable object in the memory or database with life cycle continuity, but there has to be one instance for each object. Now, let's say you are creating customers as entity objects. Each customer object would represent the restaurant guest and this cannot be used for booking orders for other guests. This may create millions of customer entity objects in the memory if millions of customers are using the system. There are not only millions of uniquely identifiable objects that exist in the system, but each object is being tracked. Both tracking and creating identity is complex. A highly credible system is required to create and track these objects, which is not only very complex but also resource heavy. It may result in system performance degradation. Therefore, it is important to use value objects instead of using entities. The reasons are explained in the next few paragraphs.

Applications don't always needs to have an identifiable customer object and be trackable. There are cases when you just need to have some or all attributes of the domain element. These are the cases when value objects can be used by the application. It makes things simple and improves the performance.

Value objects can be created and destroyed easily, owing to the absence of identity. This simplifies the design – it makes value objects available for garbage collection if no other object has referenced them.

Let's discuss the value object's immutability. Value objects should be designed and coded as immutable. Once they are created they should never be modified during their life-cycle. If you need a different value of the VO or any of its objects, then simply create a new value object, but don't modify the original value object. Here, immutability carries all the significance from **object-oriented programming** (OOP). A value object can be shared and used without impacting on its integrity if and only if it is immutable.

Frequently asked questions

1. Can a value object contain another value object?

   Yes, it can

2. Can a value object refer to another value object or entity?

   Yes, it can

3. Can I create a value object using the attributes of different value objects or entities?

   Yes, you can

Services

While creating the domain model you may encounter various situations, where behavior may not be related to any object specifically. These behaviors can be accommodated in service objects.

Ubiquitous language helps you to identify different objects, identities or value objects with different attributes and behaviors during the process of domain modeling. During the course of creating the domain model, you may find different behaviors or methods that do not belong to any specific object. Such behaviors are important so cannot be neglected. You can also not add them to entities or value objects. It would spoil the object to add behavior that does not belong to it. Keep in mind, that behavior may impact on various objects. The use of object-oriented programming makes it possible to attach to some objects; this is known as a service.

Services are common in technical frameworks. These are also used in domain layers in DDD. A service object does not have any internal state, the only purpose of it is to provide a behavior to the domain. Service objects provides behaviors that cannot be related with specific entities or value objects. Service objects may provide one or more related behaviors to one or more entities or value objects. It is a practice to define the services explicitly in the domain model.

While creating the services, you need to tick all the following points:

- Service objects' behavior performs on entities and value objects but it does not belong to entities or value objects
- Service objects' behavior state is not maintained and hence they are stateless
- Services are part of the domain model

Services may exist in other layers also. It is very important to keep domain layer services isolated. It removes the complexities and keeps the design decoupled.

Lets take an example where a restaurant owner wants to see the report of his monthly table booking. In this case, he will log in as an admin and click the **Display Report** button after providing the required input fields such as duration.

Application layers pass the request to the domain layer that owns the report and templates objects, with some parameters such as report ID and so on. Reports get created using the template and data is fetched from either the database or other sources. Then the application layer passes through all the parameters including the report ID to business layer. Here, a template needs to be fetched from the database or other source to generate the report based on the ID. This operation does not belong to either the report object or the template object. Therefore a service object is used that performs this operation to retrieve the required template from the DB.

Aggregates

Aggregate domain pattern is related to the object's life cycle and defines ownership and boundaries.

When, you reserve a table in your favorite restaurant online, using any app, you don't need to worry about the internal system and process that takes places to book your reservation such as searching the available restaurants, then the available tables during the given date, time, and so on and so forth. Therefore, you can say that a reservation app is an aggregate of several other objects and works as a root for all the other objects for a table reservation system.

This root should be an entity that binds collections of objects together. It is also called the aggregate root. This root object does not pass any reference of inside objects to external worlds and protects the changes performed in internal objects.

We need to understand why aggregators are required. A domain model can contains large numbers of domain objects. The bigger the application functionalities and size and the more complex its design, the greater number of objects will be there. A relationship exists among these objects. Some may have a many-to-many relationship, a few may have a one-to-many relationship and others may have a one-to-one relationship. These relationships are enforced by the model implementation in the code or in the database that ensures that these relationships among the objects are kept intact. Relationships are not just unidirectional, they can also be bi-directional. They can also increase in complexity.

The designer's job is to simplify these relationships in the model. Some relationships may exist in a real domain, but may not be required in the domain model. Designers need to ensure that such relationships do not exist in the domain model. Similarly, multiplicity can be reduced by these constraints. One constraint may do the job where many objects satisfy the relationship. It is also possible that a bidirectional relationship could be converted into a unidirectional relationship.

No matter how much simplification you input, you may still end up with relationships in the model. These relationships need to be maintained in the code. When one object is removed, the code should remove all the references of this object from other places. For example, a record removal from one table needs to be addressed wherever it has references in the form of foreign keys and such to keep the data consistent and maintain its integrity. Also invariants (rules) need to be forced and maintained whenever data changes.

Relationships, constraints, and invariants bring a complexity that requires an efficient handling in code. We find the solution by using the aggregate represented by the single entity known as the root that is associated with the group of objects that maintains consistency with respect to data changes.

This root is the only object that is accessible from outside, so this root element works as a boundary gate that separates the internal objects from the external world. Roots can refer to one or more inside objects and these inside objects can have references to other inside objects that may or may not have relationships with the root. However, outside objects can also refer to the root and not to any inside objects.

An aggregate ensures data integrity and enforces the invariant. Outside objects cannot make any change to inside objects they can only change the root. However, they can use the root to make a change inside the object by calling exposed operations. The root should pass the value of inside objects to outside objects if required.

If an aggregate object is stored in the database then the query should only return the aggregate object. Traversal associations should be used to return the object when it is internally linked to the aggregate root. These internal objects may also have references to other aggregates.

An aggregate root entity holds its global identity and hold local identities inside their entities.

An easy example of an aggregate in the table booking system is the customer. Customers can be exposed to external objects and their root object contains their internal object address and contact information. When requested, the value object of internal objects like address can be passed to external objects:

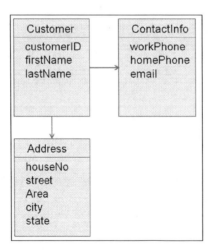

The customer as an aggregate

Repository

In a domain model, at a given point in time, many domain objects may exist. Each object may have its own life cycle from the creation of objects to their removal or persistence. Whenever any domain operation needs a domain object, it should retrieve the reference of the requested object efficiently. It would be very difficult if you didn't maintain all the available domain objects in a central object that carries the references of all the objects and is responsible for returning the requested object reference. This central object is known as the repository.

The repository is a point that interacts with infrastructures such as the database or file system. A repository object is the part of the domain model that interacts with storage such as database, external sources, and so on to retrieve the persisted objects. When a request is received by the repository for an object's reference, it returns the existing object's reference. If the requested object does not exist in the repository then it retrieves the object from storage. For example, if you need a customer, you would query the repository object to provide the customer with ID 31. The repository would provide the requested customer object if it is already available within the repository, and if not would query the persisted stores such as the database, fetch it and provide its reference.

The main advantage of using the repository is having a consistent way to retrieve objects where the requestor does not need to interact directly with the storage such as the database.

A repository may query objects from various storage types such as one or more databases, filesystems or factory repositories and so on. In such cases, a repository may have strategies that also point to different sources for different object types or categories:

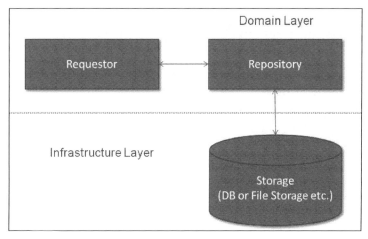

Repository object flow

As shown in the repository object flow diagram, the repository interacts with the infrastructure layer and this interface is part of the domain layer. The requestor may belong to a domain layer or an application layer. The repository helps the system to manage the life cycle of domain objects.

Factory

The factory is required when a simple constructor is not enough to create the object. It helps to create complex objects or an aggregate that involves the creation of other related objects.

A factory is also a part of the life cycle of domain objects as it is responsible for creating them. Factories and repositories are in some way related to each other as both refer to domain objects. The factory refers to newly created objects whereas the repository returns the already existing objects either from in the memory or from external storages.

Let us see how control flows using a user creation process app. Let's say that a user signs up with a username `user1`. This user creation first interacts with the factory, which creates the name `user1` and then caches it in the domain using the repository which also stores it in the storage for persistence.

When the same user logs in again, the call moves to the repository for a reference. This uses the storage to load the reference and pass it to the requestor.

The requestor may then use this `user1` object to book the table in a specified restaurant and at a specified time. These values are passed as parameters and a table booking record is created in storage using the repository:

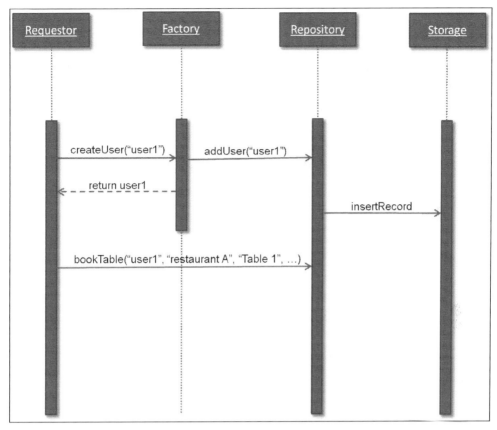

Repository object flow

The factory may use one of the object oriented programming patterns such as the factory or abstract factory pattern for object creation.

Modules

Modules are the best way of separating related business objects. These are best suited to large projects where the size of domain objects is bigger. For the end user, it makes sense to divide the domain model into modules and set the relationship between these modules. Once you understand the modules and their relationship, you start to see the bigger picture of the domain model, and it is easier to drill down further and understand the model.

Modules also help in code that is highly cohesive or that maintains low coupling. Ubiquitous language can be used to name these modules. For the table booking system, we could have different modules such as user-management, restaurants and tables, analytics and reports, and reviews, and so on.

Strategic design and principles

An enterprise model is usually very large and complex. It may be distributed among different departments in an organization. Each department may have a separate leadership team, so working and designing together can create difficulty and coordination issues. In such scenarios, maintaining the integrity of the domain model is not an easy task.

In such cases, working on a unified model is not the solution and large enterprise models need to be divided into different submodels. These submodels contain the predefined accurate relationship and contract in minute detail. Each submodel has to maintain the defined contracts without any exception.

There are various principles that could be followed to maintain the integrity of the domain model, and these are listed as follows:

- Bounded context
- Continuous integration
- Context map
    - Shared kernel
    - Customer-supplier
    - Conformist
    - Anticorruption layer
    - Separate ways
    - Open host service
    - Distillation

Bounded context

When you have different submodels, it is difficult to maintain the code when all submodels are combined. You need to have a small model that can be assigned to a single team. You might need to collect the related elements and group them. Context keeps and maintains the meaning of the domain term defined for its respective submodel by applying this set of conditions.

These domain terms defines the scope of the model that creates the boundaries of the context.

Bounded context seems very similar to the module that you learned about in the previous section. In fact, module is part of the bounded context that defines the logical frame where a submodel takes place and is developed. Whereas, the module organizes the elements of the domain model and is visible in design document and the code.

Now, as a designer you would have to keep each submodel well-defined and consistent. In this way you can refactor the each model independently without affecting the other submodels. This gives the software designer the flexibility to refine and improve it at any point in time.

Now look at the table reservation example. When you started designing the system, you would have seen that the guest would visit the app and would request a table reservation in a selected restaurant, date, and time. Then, there is backend system that informs the restaurant about the booking information, and similarly, the restaurant would keep their system updated with respect to table bookings, given that tables can also be booked by the restaurant themselves. So, when you look at the systems finer points, you can see two domains models:

- The online table reservation system
- The offline restaurant management system

Both have their own bounded context and you need to make sure that the interface between them works fine.

Continuous integration

When you are developing, the code is scattered among many teams and various technologies. This code may be organized into different modules and has applicable bounded context for respective submodels.

This sort of development may bring with it a certain level of complexity with respect to duplicate code, a code break or maybe broken-bounded context. It happens not only because of the large size of code and domain model, but also because of other factors such as changes in team members, new members or not having a well documented model to name just a few of them.

When systems are designed and developed using DDD and Agile methodologies, domain models are not designed fully before coding starts and the domain model and its elements get evolved over a period of time with continuous improvements and refinement happening over the time.

Therefore, integration continues and this is currently one of the key reasons for development today, so it plays a very important role. In continuous integration, code is merged frequently to avoid any breaks and issues with the domain model. Merged code not only gets deployed but it is also tested on a regular basis. There are various continuous integration tools available in the market that merge, build, and deploy the code at scheduled times. Organizations, these days, put more emphasis on the automation of continuous integration. Hudson, TeamCity, and Jenkins CI are a few of the popular tools available today for continuous integration. Hudson and Jenkins CI are open source tools and TeamCity is a proprietary tool.

Having a test suite attached to each build confirms the consistency and integrity of the model. A test suite defines the model from a physical point of view, whereas UML does it logically. It tells you about any error or unexpected outcome that requires a code change. It also helps to identify errors and anomalies in a domain model early.

Context map

The context map helps you to understand the overall picture of a large enterprise application. It shows how many bounded contexts are present in the enterprise model and how they are interrelated. Therefore we can say that any diagram or document that explains the bounded contexts and relationship between them is called a context map.

Context maps helps all team members, whether they are in the same team or in different team, to understand the high-level enterprise model in the form of various parts (bounded context or submodels) and relationships. This gives individuals a clearer picture about the tasks one performs and may allow him to raise any concern/question about the model's integrity:

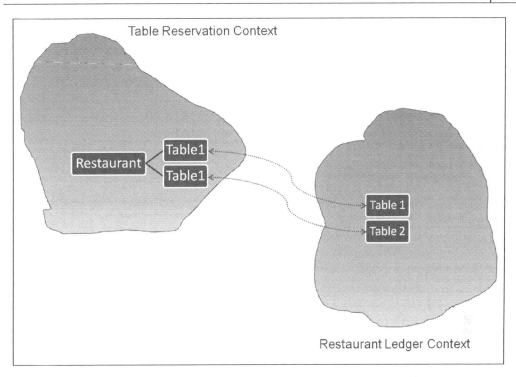

Context map example

The context map example diagram is a sample of a context map. Here, **Table1** and **Table2** both appear in the **Table Reservation Context** and also in the **Restaurant Ledger Context**. The interesting thing is that **Table1** and **Table2** have their own respective concept in each bounded context. Here, ubiquitous language is used to name the bounded context as table reservation and restaurant ledger.

In the following section, we will explore a few patterns that can be used to define the communication between different contexts in the context map.

Shared kernel

As the name suggests, one part of the bounded context is shared with the other's bounded context. As you can see below the **Restaurant** entity is being shared between the **Table Reservation Context** and the **Restaurant Ledger Context**:

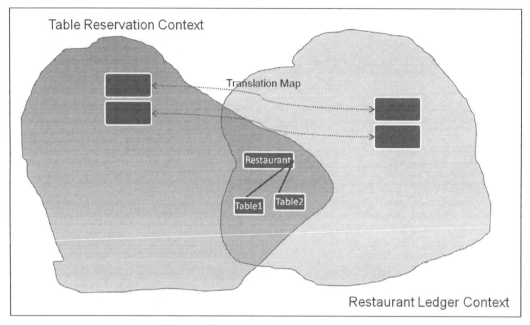

Shared kernel

Customer-supplier

The customer-supplier pattern represents the relationship between two bounded contexts when the output of one bounded context is required for the other bounded context that is, one supplies the information to the other (known as the customer) who consumes the information.

In a real world example, a car dealer could not sell cars until the car manufacturer delivers them. Hence, in this domain-model, the car manufacturer is the supplier and the dealer is the customer. This relationship establishes a customer-supplier relationship because the output (car) of one bounded context (car-manufacturer) is required by the other bounded context (dealer).

Here, both customer and supplier teams should meet regularly to establish a contract and form the right protocol to communicate with each other.

Conformist

This pattern is similar to that of the customer and the supplier, where one needs to provide the contract and information while the other needs to use it. Here, instead of bounded context, actual teams are involved in having an upstream/downstream relationship.

Moreover, upstream teams do not provide for the needs of the downstream team because of their lack of motivation. Therefore, it is possible that the downstream team may need to plan and work on items which will never be available. To resolve such cases, either the customer team could develop their own models if the supplier provides information that is not worth enough. If the supplier provided information is really of worth or of partial worth, then the customer can use the interface or translators that can be used to consume the supplier-provided information with the customer's own models.

Anticorruption layer

The anticorruption layer remains part of a domain and it is used when a system needs data from external systems or from their own legacy systems. Here, anticorruption is the layer that interacts with external systems and uses external system data in the domain model without affecting the integrity and originality of the domain model.

For the most part, a service can be used as an anticorruption layer that may use a facade pattern with an adapter and translator to consume external domain data within the internal model. Therefore, your system would always use the service to retrieve the data. The service layer can be designed using the façade pattern. This would make sure that it would work with the domain model to provide the required data in a given format. The service could then also use the adapter and translator patterns that would make sure that whatever format and hierarchy the data is sent in, by external sources, the service would be provided in a desired format and the hierarchy would use adapters and translators.

Separate ways

When you have a large enterprise application and a domain where different domains have no common elements and it's made of large submodels that can work independently, this still works as a single application for an end user.

In such cases, a designer could create separate models that have no relationship and develop a small application on top of them. These small applications become a single application when merged together.

An employer's Intranet application that offers various small applications such as those that are HR-related, issue trackers, transport or intra-company social networks, is one such application where a designer could use the separate ways pattern.

It would be very challenging and complex to integrate applications that were developed using separate models. Therefore, you should take care before implementing this pattern.

Open host service

A translation layer is used when two submodels interact with each other. This translation layer is used when you integrate models with an external system. This works fine when you have one submodel that uses this external system. The open host service is required when this external system is being used by many submodels to remove the extra and duplicated code because then you need to write a translation layer for each submodel external system.

An open host service provides the services of an external system using a wrapper to all sub-models.

Distillation

As you know, distillation is the process of purifying liquid. Similarly, in DDD, distillation is the process that filters out the information that is not required, and keeps only the meaningful information. It helps you to identify the core domain and the essential concepts for your business domain. It helps you to filter out the generic concepts until you get the code domain concept.

Core domain should be designed, developed and implemented with the highest attention to detail, using the developers and designers, as it is crucial for the success of the whole system.

In our table reservation system example, which is not a large, or a complex domain application, it is not difficult to identify the core domain. The core domain here exists to share the real-time accurate vacant tables in the restaurants and allows the user to reserve them in a hassle free process.

Sample domain service

Let us create a sample domain service based on our table reservation system. As discussed in this chapter, the importance of an efficient domain layer is the key to successful products or services. Projects developed based on the domain layer are more maintainable, highly cohesive, and decoupled. They provide high scalability in terms of business requirement change and have a low impact on the design of other layers.

Domain-driven development is based on domain, hence it is not recommended that you use a top-down approach where the UI would be developed first, followed by the rest of the layers and finally the persistence layer, or a bottom-up approach where the persistence layer like the DB is designed first and then the rest of the layers, with the UI at last.

Having a domain model developed first, using the patterns described in this book, gives clarity to all team members functionality wise and an advantage to the software designer to build a flexible, maintainable and consistent system that helps the organization to launch a world class product with less maintenance costs.

Here, you will create a restaurant service that provides the feature to add and retrieve restaurants. Based on implementation, you can add other functionalities such as finding restaurants based on cuisine or on rating.

Start with the entity. Here, the restaurant is our entity as each restaurant is unique and has an identifier. You can use an interface or set of interfaces to implement the entity in our table reservation system. Ideally, if you go by the interface segregation principle, you will use a set of interfaces rather than a single interface.

 The **Interface Segregation Principle (ISP)**: clients should not be forced to depend upon interfaces that they do not use.

Entity implementation

For the first interface you could have an abstract class or interface that is required by all the entities. For example if we consider ID and name, attributes would be common for all entities. Therefore, you could use the abstract class `Entity` as an abstraction of entity in your domain layer:

```
public abstract class Entity<T> {

    T id;
    String name;

}
```

Based on that you can also have another abstract class that inherits `Entity`, an abstract class:

```
public abstract class BaseEntity<T> extends Entity<T> {

    private T id;
```

```
        public BaseEntity(T id, String name) {
            super.id = id;
            super.name = name;

        }
        ... (getter/setter and other relevant code)
    }
```

Based on the preceding abstractions, we could create the `Restaurant` entity for restaurant management.

Now since we are developing the table reservation system, `Table` is another important entity in terms of the domain model. So, if we go by the aggregate pattern, `restaurant` would work as a root, and table would be internal to the `Restaurant` entity. Therefore, the `Table` entity would always be accessible using the `Restaurant` entity.

You can create the `Table` entity using the following implementation, and you can add attributes as you wish. For demonstration purpose only, basic attributes are used:

```
public class Table extends BaseEntity<BigInteger> {

    private int capacity;

    public Table(String name, BigInteger id, int capacity) {
        super(id, name);
        this.capacity = capacity;
    }

    public void setCapacity(int capacity) {
        this.capacity = capacity;
    }

    public int getCapacity() {
        return capacity;
    }
}
```

Now, we can implement the aggregator `Restaurant` shown as follows. Here, only basic attributes are used. You could add as many you want or may add other features also:

```
public class Restaurant extends BaseEntity<String> {

    private List<Table> tables = new ArrayList<>();
```

```
public Restaurant(String name, String id, List<Table> tables) {
    super(id, name);
    this.tables = tables;
}

public void setTables(List<Table> tables) {
    this.tables = tables;
}

public List<Table> getTables() {
    return tables;
}
}
```

Repository implementation

Now, we can implement the repository pattern as learned in this chapter. To start with, you will first create the two interfaces `Repository` and `ReadOnlyRepository`. `ReadOnlyRepository` will be used to provide abstraction for read only operations whereas `Repository` abstraction will be used to perform all types of operations:

```
public interface ReadOnlyRepository<TE, T> {

    boolean contains(T id);

    Entity get(T id);

    Collection<TE> getAll();
}
```

Based on this interface, we could create the abstraction of the repository that would do additional operations such as adding, removing, and updating:

```
public interface Repository<TE, T> extends ReadOnlyRepository<TE, T> {

    void add(TE entity);

    void remove(T id);

    void update(TE entity);
}
```

Repository abstraction as defined previously could be implemented in a way that suits you to persist your objects. The change in persistence code, that is a part of infrastructure layer, won't impact on your domain layer code as the contract and abstraction are defined by the domain layer. The domain layer uses the abstraction classes and interfaces that remove the use of direct concrete class and provides the loose coupling. For demonstration purpose, we could simple use the map that remains in the memory to persist the objects:

```java
public interface RestaurantRepository<Restaurant, String> extends
Repository<Restaurant, String> {

    boolean ContainsName(String name);
}


public class InMemRestaurantRepository implements RestaurantRepository
<Restaurant, String> {

    private Map<String, Restaurant> entities;

    public InMemRestaurantRepository() {
        entities = new HashMap();
    }

    @Override
    public boolean ContainsName(String name) {
        return entities.containsKey(name);
    }

    @Override
    public void add(Restaurant entity) {
        entities.put(entity.getName(), entity);
    }

    @Override
    public void remove(String id) {
        if (entities.containsKey(id)) {
            entities.remove(id);
        }
    }

    @Override
    public void update(Restaurant entity) {
        if (entities.containsKey(entity.getName())) {
            entities.put(entity.getName(), entity);
```

```
            }
    }

    @Override
    public boolean contains(String id) {
        throw new UnsupportedOperationException("Not supported yet.");
    //To change body of generated methods, choose Tools | Templates.
    }

    @Override
    public Entity get(String id) {
        throw new UnsupportedOperationException("Not supported yet.");
    //To change body of generated methods, choose Tools | Templates.
    }

    @Override
    public Collection<Restaurant> getAll() {
        return entities.values();
    }

}
```

Service implementation

In the same way as the preceding approach, you could divide the abstraction of domain service into two parts: main service abstraction and read only service abstraction:

```
public abstract class ReadOnlyBaseService<TE, T> {

    private Repository<TE, T> repository;

    ReadOnlyBaseService(Repository<TE, T> repository) {
        this.repository = repository;
    }
    ...
}
```

Now, we could use this ReadOnlyBaseService to create the BaseService. Here, we are using the dependency inject pattern via a constructor to map the concrete objects with abstraction:

```
public abstract class BaseService<TE, T> extends
ReadOnlyBaseService<TE, T> {
```

```java
    private Repository<TE, T> _repository;

    BaseService(Repository<TE, T> repository) {
        super(repository);
        _repository = repository;
    }

    public void add(TE entity) throws Exception {
        _repository.add(entity);
    }

    public Collection<TE> getAll() {
        return _repository.getAll();
    }
}
```

Now, after defining the service abstraction services, we could implement the `RestaurantService` in the following way:

```java
public class RestaurantService extends BaseService<Restaurant,
BigInteger> {

    private RestaurantRepository<Restaurant, String>
restaurantRepository;

    public RestaurantService(RestaurantRepository repository) {
        super(repository);
        restaurantRepository = repository;
    }

    public void add(Restaurant restaurant) throws Exception {
        if (restaurantRepository.ContainsName(restaurant.getName())) {
            throw new Exception(String.format("There is already a
product with the name - %s", restaurant.getName()));
        }

        if (restaurant.getName() == null || "".equals(restaurant.
getName())) {
            throw new Exception("Restaurant name cannot be null or
empty string.");
        }
        super.add(restaurant);
    }
}
```

Similarly, you could write the implementation for other entities. This code is a basic implementation and you might add various implementations and behaviors in the production code.

Summary

In this chapter, you have learned the fundamentals of DDD. You have also explored multilayered architecture and different patterns one can use to develop software using DDD. By this time, you might be aware that the domain model design is very important for the success of the software. At the end, there is also one domain service implementation shown using the restaurant table reservation system.

In the next chapter, you will learn how to use the design is used to implement the sample project. The explanation of the design of this sample project is derived from the last chapter and the DDD will be used to build the microservices. This chapter not only covers the coding, but also the different aspects of the microservices such as build, unit-testing, and packaging. At the end of the next chapter, the sample microservice project will be ready for deployment and consumption.

Implementing a Microservice

This chapter takes you from the design stage to the implementation of our sample project – an **Online Table Reservation System (OTRS)**. Here, you will use the same design explained in the last chapter and enhance it to build the μService. At the end of this chapter, you will not only have learned to implement the design, but also learned the different aspects of μServices – building, testing, and packaging. Although the focus is on building and implementing the Restaurant μService, you can use the same approach to build and implement other μServices used in the OTRS.

In this chapter, we will cover the following topics:

- OTRS overview
- Developing and implementing μService
- Testing

We will use the domain-driven design key concepts demonstrated in the last chapter. In the last chapter, you saw how domain-driven design is used to develop the domain model using core Java. Now, we will move from a sample domain implementation to a Spring framework-driven implementation. You'll make use of Spring Boot to implement the domain-driven design concepts and transform them from core Java to a Spring framework-based model.

In addition, we'll also use the Spring Cloud, which provides a cloud-ready solution. Spring Cloud also uses Spring Boot, which allows you to use an embedded application container relying on Tomcat or Jetty inside your service, which is packages as a JAR or as a WAR. This JAR is executed as a separate process, a μService that would serve and provide the response to all requests and, point to endpoints defined in the service.

Spring Cloud can also be integrated easily with Netflix Eureka, a service registry and discovery component. The OTRS will use it for registration and the discovery of μServices.

OTRS overview

Based on µService principles, we need to have separate µServices for each functionality that can function independently. After looking at the OTRS, we can easily divide the OTRS into three main µServices – Restaurant service, Booking service, and User service. There can be other µServices that can be defined in the OTRS. Our focus is on these three µServices. The idea is to make them independent, including having their own separate databases.

We can summarize the functionalities of these services as follows:

- **Restaurant service**: This service provides the functionality for the Restaurant resource – **create, read, update, delete (CRUD)** operation and searching based on criteria. It provides the association between restaurants and tables. Restaurant would also provide the access to the Table entity.

- **User service**: This service, as the name suggests, allows the end user to perform CRUD operations on User entities.

- **Booking service**: This makes use of the Restaurant service and User service to perform CRUD operations on booking. It would use the Restaurant searching, its associated tables lookup and allocation based on table availability for a specified time duration. It creates the relationship between the Restaurant/ Table and the User.

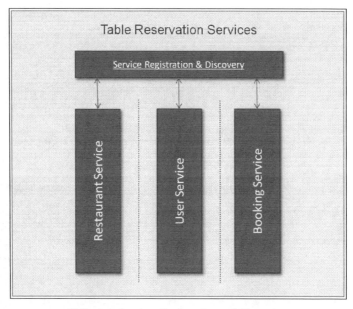

Different µServices, Registration and Discovery

The preceding diagram shows how each μService works independently. This is the reason μServices can be developed, enhanced, and maintained separately, without affecting others. These services can each have their own layered architecture and database. There is no restriction to use same technologies, frameworks, and languages to develop these services. At any given point in time, you can also introduce new μServices. For example, for accounting purposes, we can introduce an accounting service that can be exposed to Restaurant for book keeping. Similarly, analytics and reporting are other services that can be integrated and exposed.

For demonstration purposes, we will only implement the three services shown in the preceding diagram.

Developing and implementing μServices

We will use the domain-driven implementation and approach described in the last chapter to implement the μServices using Spring Cloud. Let's revisit the key artifacts:

- **Entities**: These are categories of objects that are identifiable and remain the same throughout the states of the product/services. These objects are NOT defined by their attributes, but by their identities and threads of continuity.

  Entities have traits such as identity, a thread of continuity, and attributes that do not define their identity. **Value Objects (VO)** just have the attributes and no conceptual identity. A best practice is to keep Value Objects as immutable objects. In the Spring framework, entities are pure POJOs, therefore we'll also use them as VO.

- **Services**: These are common in technical frameworks. These are also used in the Domain layer in domain-driven design. A Service object does not have an internal state; the only purpose of it is to provide the behavior to the domain. Service objects provide behaviors that cannot be related with specific entities or value objects. Service objects may provide one or more related behaviors to one or more entities or value objects. It is a best practice to define the Services explicitly in the domain model.

- **Repository object**: A Repository object is a part of the domain model that interacts with storage, such as databases, external sources and so on, to retrieve the persisted objects. When a request is received by the repository for an object reference, it returns the existing object reference. If the requested object does not exist in the repository, then it retrieves the object from storage.

- Each OTRS μService API represents a RESTful web service. The OTRS API uses HTTP verbs such as GET, POST, and so on, and a RESTful endpoint structure. Request and response payloads are formatted as JSON. If required, XML can also be used.

Restaurant μService

The Restaurant μService will be exposed to the external world using REST endpoints for consumption. We'll find the following endpoints in the Restaurant μService example. One can add as many endpoints as per the requirements:

Endpoint	GET /v1/restaurants/<Restaurant-Id>	
Parameters		
Name	**Description**	
Restaurant_Id	Path parameter that represents the unique restaurant associated with this ID	
Request		
Property	**Type**	**Description**
None		
Response		
Property	**Type**	**Description**
Restaurant	Restaurant object	Restaurant object that is associated with the given ID

Endpoint	GET /v1/restaurants/	
Parameters		
Name	**Description**	
None		
Request		
Property	**Type**	**Description**
Name	String	Query parameter that represents the name, or substring of the name, of the restaurant
Response		
Property	**Type**	**Description**
Restaurants	Array of restaurant objects	Returns all the restaurants whose names contain the given name value

Endpoint	POST /v1/restaurants/	
Parameters		
Name	**Description**	
None		
Request		
Property	**Type**	**Description**
Restaurant	Restaurant object	A JSON representation of the restaurant object
Response		
Property	**Type**	**Description**
Restaurant	Restaurant object	A newly created Restaurant object

Similarly, we can add various endpoints and their implementations. For demonstration purposes, we'll implement the preceding endpoints using Spring Cloud.

Controller class

The Restaurant Controller uses the @RestController annotation to build the restaurant service endpoints. We have already gone through the details of @RestController in *Chapter 2, Setting Up the Development Environment*. @RestController is a class-level annotation that is used for resource classes. It is a combination of @Controller and @ResponseBody. It returns the domain object.

API versioning

As we move forward, I would like to share with you that we are using the v1 prefix on our REST endpoint. That represents the version of the API. I would also like to brief you on the importance of API versioning. Versioning APIs is important, because APIs change over time. Your knowledge and experience improves with time, which leads to changes to your API. A change of API may break existing client integrations.

Therefore, there are various ways of managing API versions. One of these is using the version in path or some use the HTTP header. The HTTP header can be a custom request header or an Accept header to represent the calling API version. Please refer to *RESTful Java Patterns and Best Practices* by Bhakti Mehta, Packt Publishing, https://www.packtpub.com/application-development/restful-java-patterns-and-best-practices, for more information.

```
@RestController
@RequestMapping("/v1/restaurants")
public class RestaurantController {

    protected Logger logger = Logger.getLogger(RestaurantController.
class.getName());

    protected RestaurantService restaurantService;

    @Autowired
    public RestaurantController(RestaurantService restaurantService) {
        this.restaurantService = restaurantService;
    }

    /**
     * Fetch restaurants with the specified name. A partial case-
insensitive
     * match is supported. So <code>http://.../restaurants/rest</code>
will find
     * any restaurants with upper or lower case 'rest' in their name.
     *
     * @param name
```

```
     * @return A non-null, non-empty collection of restaurants.
     */
    @RequestMapping(method = RequestMethod.GET)
    public ResponseEntity<Collection<Restaurant>> findByName(@
RequestParam("name") String name) {

logger.info(String.format("restaurant-service findByName() invoked:{}
for {} ", restaurantService.getClass().getName(), name));
        name = name.trim().toLowerCase();
        Collection<Restaurant> restaurants;
        try {
            restaurants = restaurantService.findByName(name);
        } catch (Exception ex) {
            logger.log(Level.WARNING, "Exception raised findByName
REST Call", ex);
            return new ResponseEntity< Collection<
Restaurant>>(HttpStatus.INTERNAL_SERVER_ERROR);
        }
        return restaurants.size() > 0 ? new ResponseEntity<
Collection< Restaurant>>(restaurants, HttpStatus.OK)
                : new ResponseEntity< Collection<
Restaurant>>(HttpStatus.NO_CONTENT);
    }


    /**
     * Fetch restaurants with the given id.
     * <code>http://.../v1/restaurants/{restaurant_id}</code> will
return
     * restaurant with given id.
     *
     * @param retaurant_id
     * @return A non-null, non-empty collection of restaurants.
     */
    @RequestMapping(value = "/{restaurant_id}", method =
RequestMethod.GET)
    public ResponseEntity<Entity> findById(@PathVariable("restaurant_
id") String id) {

        logger.info(String.format("restaurant-service findById()
invoked:{} for {} ", restaurantService.getClass().getName(), id));
        id = id.trim();
        Entity restaurant;
        try {
            restaurant = restaurantService.findById(id);
```

```
        } catch (Exception ex) {
            logger.log(Level.SEVERE, "Exception raised findById REST
Call", ex);
            return new ResponseEntity<Entity>(HttpStatus.INTERNAL_
SERVER_ERROR);
        }
        return restaurant != null ? new ResponseEntity<Entity>(restaur
ant, HttpStatus.OK)
                : new ResponseEntity<Entity>(HttpStatus.NO_CONTENT);
    }


    /**
     * Add restaurant with the specified information.
     *
     * @param Restaurant
     * @return A non-null restaurant.
     * @throws RestaurantNotFoundException If there are no matches at
all.
     */
    @RequestMapping(method = RequestMethod.POST)
    public ResponseEntity<Restaurant> add(@RequestBody RestaurantVO
restaurantVO) {

        logger.info(String.format("restaurant-service add() invoked:
%s for %s", restaurantService.getClass().getName(), restaurantVO.
getName()));

        Restaurant restaurant = new Restaurant(null, null, null);
        BeanUtils.copyProperties(restaurantVO, restaurant);
        try {
            restaurantService.add(restaurant);
        } catch (Exception ex) {
            logger.log(Level.WARNING, "Exception raised add Restaurant
REST Call "+ ex);
            return new ResponseEntity<Restaurant>(HttpStatus.
UNPROCESSABLE_ENTITY);
        }
        return new ResponseEntity<Restaurant>(HttpStatus.CREATED);
    }
}
```

Service classes

`RestaurantController` **uses** `RestaurantService`. `RestaurantService` is an interface that defines CRUD and some search operations and is defined as follows:

```
public interface RestaurantService {

    public void add(Restaurant restaurant) throws Exception;

    public void update(Restaurant restaurant) throws Exception;

    public void delete(String id) throws Exception;

    public Entity findById(String restaurantId) throws Exception;

    public Collection<Restaurant> findByName(String name) throws
Exception;

    public Collection<Restaurant> findByCriteria(Map<String,
ArrayList<String>> name) throws Exception;
}
```

Now, we can implement the `RestaurantService` we have just defined. It also extends the `BaseService` you created in the last chapter. We use `@Service` Spring annotation to define it as a service:

```
@Service("restaurantService")
public class RestaurantServiceImpl extends BaseService<Restaurant,
String>
        implements RestaurantService {

    private RestaurantRepository<Restaurant, String>
restaurantRepository;

    @Autowired
    public RestaurantServiceImpl(RestaurantRepository<Restaurant,
String> restaurantRepository) {
        super(restaurantRepository);
        this.restaurantRepository = restaurantRepository;
    }

    public void add(Restaurant restaurant) throws Exception {
        if (restaurant.getName() == null || "".equals(restaurant.
getName())) {
```

```
                throw new Exception("Restaurant name cannot be null or
empty string.");
        }

        if (restaurantRepository.containsName(restaurant.getName())) {
            throw new Exception(String.format("There is already a
product with the name - %s", restaurant.getName()));
        }

        super.add(restaurant);
    }

    @Override
    public Collection<Restaurant> findByName(String name) throws
Exception {
        return restaurantRepository.findByName(name);
    }

    @Override
    public void update(Restaurant restaurant) throws Exception {
        restaurantRepository.update(restaurant);
    }

    @Override
    public void delete(String id) throws Exception {
        restaurantRepository.remove(id);
    }

    @Override
    public Entity findById(String restaurantId) throws Exception {
        return restaurantRepository.get(restaurantId);
    }

    @Override
    public Collection<Restaurant> findByCriteria(Map<String,
ArrayList<String>> name) throws Exception {
        throw new UnsupportedOperationException("Not supported yet.");
//To change body of generated methods, choose Tools | Templates.
    }
}
```

Repository classes

The `RestaurantRepository` interface defines two new methods: the `containsName` and `findByName` methods. It also extends the `Repository` interface:

```
public interface RestaurantRepository<Restaurant, String> extends
Repository<Restaurant, String> {

    boolean containsName(String name) throws Exception;

    Collection<Restaurant> findByName(String name) throws Exception;
}
```

The `Repository` interface defines three methods: `add`, `remove`, and `update`. It also extends the `ReadOnlyRepository` interface:

```
public interface Repository<TE, T> extends ReadOnlyRepository<TE, T> {

    void add(TE entity);

    void remove(T id);

    void update(TE entity);
}
```

The `ReadOnlyRepository` interface definition contains the `get` and `getAll` methods, which return Boolean values, Entity, and collection of Entity respectively. It is useful if you want to expose only a read-only abstraction of the repository:

```
public interface ReadOnlyRepository<TE, T> {

    boolean contains(T id);

    Entity get(T id);

    Collection<TE> getAll();
}
```

Spring framework makes use of the `@Repository` annotation to define the repository bean that implements the repository. In the case of `RestaurantRepository`, you can see that a map is used in place of the actual database implementation. This keeps all entities saved in memory only. Therefore, when we start the service, we find only two restaurants in memory. We can use JPA for database persistence. This is the general practice for production-ready implementations:

```
@Repository("restaurantRepository")
public class InMemRestaurantRepository implements RestaurantRepository
<Restaurant, String> {
```

```java
        private Map<String, Restaurant> entities;

    public InMemRestaurantRepository() {
        entities = new HashMap();
        Restaurant restaurant = new Restaurant("Big-O Restaurant",
"1", null);
        entities.put("1", restaurant);
        restaurant = new Restaurant("O Restaurant", "2", null);
        entities.put("2", restaurant);
    }


    @Override
    public boolean containsName(String name) {
        try {
            return this.findByName(name).size() > 0;
        } catch (Exception ex) {
            //Exception Handler
        }
        return false;
    }


    @Override
    public void add(Restaurant entity) {
        entities.put(entity.getId(), entity);
    }


    @Override
    public void remove(String id) {
        if (entities.containsKey(id)) {
            entities.remove(id);
        }
    }


    @Override
    public void update(Restaurant entity) {
        if (entities.containsKey(entity.getId())) {
            entities.put(entity.getId(), entity);
        }
    }


    @Override
    public Collection<Restaurant> findByName(String name) throws
Exception {
        Collection<Restaurant> restaurants = new ArrayList();
```

```
        int noOfChars = name.length();
        entities.forEach((k, v) -> {
            if (v.getName().toLowerCase().contains(name.subSequence(0,
noOfChars))) {
                restaurants.add(v);
            }
        });
        return restaurants;
    }


    @Override
    public boolean contains(String id) {
        throw new UnsupportedOperationException("Not supported yet.");
//To change body of generated methods, choose Tools | Templates.
    }

    @Override
    public Entity get(String id) {
        return entities.get(id);
    }

    @Override
    public Collection<Restaurant> getAll() {
        return entities.values();
    }
}
```

Entity classes

The Restaurant entity, which extends BaseEntity, is defined as follows:

```
public class Restaurant extends BaseEntity<String> {

    private List<Table> tables = new ArrayList<>();

    public Restaurant(String name, String id, List<Table> tables) {
        super(id, name);
        this.tables = tables;
    }

    public void setTables(List<Table> tables) {
        this.tables = tables;
    }

    public List<Table> getTables() {
```

```
            return tables;
    }


    @Override
    public String toString() {
        StringBuilder sb = new StringBuilder();
        sb.append(String.format("id: {}, name: {}, capacity: {}",
this.getId(), this.getName(), this.getCapacity()));
        return sb.toString();
    }


}
```

 Since, we are using POJO classes for our entity definitions, we do not need to create a Value object in many cases. The idea is that the state of the object should not be persisted across.

The Table entity, which extends BaseEntity, is defined as follows:

```
public class Table extends BaseEntity<BigInteger> {

    private int capacity;

    public Table(String name, BigInteger id, int capacity) {
        super(id, name);
        this.capacity = capacity;
    }

    public void setCapacity(int capacity) {
        this.capacity = capacity;
    }

    public int getCapacity() {
        return capacity;
    }

    @Override
    public String toString() {
        StringBuilder sb = new StringBuilder();
        sb.append(String.format("id: {}, name: {}", this.getId(),
this.getName()));
        sb.append(String.format("Tables: {}" + Arrays.asList(this.
getTables())));
        return sb.toString();
    }


}
```

The `Entity` abstract class is defined as follows:

```
public abstract class Entity<T> {

    T id;
    String name;

    public T getId() {
        return id;
    }

    public void setId(T id) {
        this.id = id;
    }

    public String getName() {
        return name;
    }

    public void setName(String name) {
        this.name = name;
    }

}
```

The `BaseEntity` abstract class is defined as follows. It extends the `Entity` abstract class:

```
public abstract class BaseEntity<T> extends Entity<T> {

    private T id;
    private boolean isModified;
    private String name;

    public BaseEntity(T id, String name) {
        this.id = id;
        this.name = name;
    }

    public T getId() {
        return id;
    }

    public void setId(T id) {
        this.id = id;
```

```
    }

    public boolean isIsModified() {
        return isModified;
    }

    public void setIsModified(boolean isModified) {
        this.isModified = isModified;
    }

    public String getName() {
        return name;
    }

    public void setName(String name) {
        this.name = name;
    }

}
```

Booking and user services

We can use the RestaurantService implementation to develop the Booking and User services. The User service can offer the endpoint related to the User resource with respect to CRUD operations. The Booking service can offer the endpoints related to the Booking resource with respect to CRUD operations and the availability of table slots. You can find the sample code of these services on the Packt website.

Registration and Discovery service (Eureka service)

Spring Cloud provides state-of-the-art support to *Netflix Eureka*, a service registry and discovery tool. All services executed by you get listed and discovered by Eureka service, which it reads from the Eureka client Spring configuration inside your service project.

It needs a Spring Cloud dependency as shown here and a startup class with the @EnableEurekaApplication annotation in pom.xml:

Maven dependency:

```
<dependency>
  <groupId>org.springframework.cloud</groupId>
  <artifactId>spring-cloud-starter-eureka-server</artifactId>
</dependency>
```

Startup class:

The startup class **App** would run the Eureka service seamlessly by just using the
`@EnableEurekaApplication` class annotation:

```
package com.packtpub.mmj.eureka.service;

import org.springframework.boot.SpringApplication;
import org.springframework.boot.autoconfigure.SpringBootApplication;
import org.springframework.cloud.netflix.eureka.server.
EnableEurekaServer;

@SpringBootApplication
@EnableEurekaServer
public class App {

    public static void main(String[] args) {
        SpringApplication.run(App.class, args);
    }
}
```

 Use `<start-class>com.packtpub.mmj.eureka.service.App</start-class>` under the `<properties>` tag in the `pom.xml` project.

Spring configurations:

Eureka Service also needs the following Spring configuration for Eureka Server
configuration (`src/main/resources/application.yml`):

```
server:
  port: ${vcap.application.port:8761}    # HTTP port

eureka:
  instance:
    hostname: localhost
  client:
    registerWithEureka: false
    fetchRegistry: false
  server:
    waitTimeInMsWhenSyncEmpty: 0
```

Similar to Eureka Server, each OTRS service should also contain the Eureka Client
configuration, so that a connection between Eureka Server and the client can be
established. Without this, the registration and discovery of services is not possible.

Eureka Client: your services can use the following spring configuration to configure Eureka Server:

```
eureka:
  client:
    serviceUrl:
      defaultZone: http://localhost:8761/eureka/
```

Execution

To see how our code works, we need to first build it and then execute it. We'll use Maven *clean package* to build the service JARs.

Now to execute these service JARs, simply execute the following command from the service home directory:

```
java -jar target/<service_jar_file>
```

For example:

```
java -jar target/restaurant-service.jar
java -jar target/eureka-service.jar
```

Testing

To enable testing, add the following dependency in pom.xml:

```
<dependency>
    <groupId>org.springframework.boot</groupId>
    <artifactId>spring-boot-starter-test</artifactId>
</dependency>
```

To test the RestaurantController, the following files have been added:

*   RestaurantControllerIntegrationTests, which uses the @SpringApplicationConfiguration annotation to pick the same configuration that Spring Boot uses:

    ```
    @RunWith(SpringJUnit4ClassRunner.class)
    @SpringApplicationConfiguration(classes = RestaurantApp.class)
    public class RestaurantControllerIntegrationTests extends
            AbstractRestaurantControllerTests {

    }
    ```

- An abstract class to write our tests:

```
public abstract class AbstractRestaurantControllerTests {

    protected static final String RESTAURANT = "1";
    protected static final String RESTAURANT_NAME = "Big-O
Restaurant";

    @Autowired
    RestaurantController restaurantController;

    @Test
    public void validResturantById() {
        Logger.getGlobal().info("Start validResturantById test");
        ResponseEntity<Entity> restaurant = restaurantController.
findById(RESTAURANT);

        Assert.assertEquals(HttpStatus.OK, restaurant.
getStatusCode());
        Assert.assertTrue(restaurant.hasBody());
        Assert.assertNotNull(restaurant.getBody());
        Assert.assertEquals(RESTAURANT, restaurant.getBody().
getId());
        Assert.assertEquals(RESTAURANT_NAME, restaurant.getBody().
getName());
        Logger.getGlobal().info("End validResturantById test");
    }

    @Test
    public void validResturantByName() {
        Logger.getGlobal().info("Start validResturantByName
test");
        ResponseEntity<Collection<Restaurant>> restaurants =
restaurantController.findByName(RESTAURANT_NAME);
        Logger.getGlobal().info("In validAccount test");

        Assert.assertEquals(HttpStatus.OK, restaurants.
getStatusCode());
        Assert.assertTrue(restaurants.hasBody());
        Assert.assertNotNull(restaurants.getBody());
        Assert.assertFalse(restaurants.getBody().isEmpty());
        Restaurant restaurant = (Restaurant) restaurants.
getBody().toArray()[0];
        Assert.assertEquals(RESTAURANT, restaurant.getId());
        Assert.assertEquals(RESTAURANT_NAME, restaurant.
getName());
```

```
            Logger.getGlobal().info("End validResturantByName test");
        }


        @Test
        public void validAdd() {
            Logger.getGlobal().info("Start validAdd test");
            RestaurantVO restaurant = new RestaurantVO();
            restaurant.setId("999");
            restaurant.setName("Test Restaurant");

            ResponseEntity<Restaurant> restaurants =
restaurantController.add(restaurant);
            Assert.assertEquals(HttpStatus.CREATED, restaurants.
getStatusCode());
            Logger.getGlobal().info("End validAdd test");
        }
}
```

- Finally, RestaurantControllerTests, which extends the previously created abstract class and also creates the RestaurantService and RestaurantRepository implementations:

```
public class RestaurantControllerTests extends
AbstractRestaurantControllerTests {

    protected static final Restaurant restaurantStaticInstance =
new Restaurant(RESTAURANT,
            RESTAURANT_NAME, null);

    protected static class TestRestaurantRepository implements Res
taurantRepository<Restaurant, String> {

        private Map<String, Restaurant> entities;

        public TestRestaurantRepository() {
            entities = new HashMap();
            Restaurant restaurant = new Restaurant("Big-O
Restaurant", "1", null);
            entities.put("1", restaurant);
            restaurant = new Restaurant("O Restaurant", "2",
null);
            entities.put("2", restaurant);
        }

        @Override
        public boolean containsName(String name) {
            try {
                return this.findByName(name).size() > 0;
```

```
        } catch (Exception ex) {
            //Exception Handler
        }
        return false;
    }

    @Override
    public void add(Restaurant entity) {
        entities.put(entity.getId(), entity);
    }

    @Override
    public void remove(String id) {
        if (entities.containsKey(id)) {
            entities.remove(id);
        }
    }

    @Override
    public void update(Restaurant entity) {
        if (entities.containsKey(entity.getId())) {
            entities.put(entity.getId(), entity);
        }
    }

    @Override
    public Collection<Restaurant> findByName(String name)
throws Exception {
        Collection<Restaurant> restaurants = new ArrayList();
        int noOfChars = name.length();
        entities.forEach((k, v) -> {
            if (v.getName().toLowerCase().contains(name.
subSequence(0, noOfChars))) {
                restaurants.add(v);
            }
        });
        return restaurants;
    }

    @Override
    public boolean contains(String id) {
        throw new UnsupportedOperationException("Not supported
yet."); //To change body of generated methods, choose Tools |
Templates.
    }

    @Override
    public Entity get(String id) {
        return entities.get(id);
    }
```

```
        @Override
        public Collection<Restaurant> getAll() {
            return entities.values();
        }
    }

    protected TestRestaurantRepository testRestaurantRepository =
new TestRestaurantRepository();
    protected RestaurantService restaurantService = new Restaurant
ServiceImpl(testRestaurantRepository);

    @Before
    public void setup() {
        restaurantController = new RestaurantController(restaurant
Service);

    }
}
```

References

- *RESTful Java Patterns and Best Practices* by Bhakti Mehta, Packt Publishing: https://www.packtpub.com/application-development/restful-java-patterns-and-best-practices

- *Spring Cloud*: http://cloud.spring.io/

- *Netflix Eureka*: https://github.com/netflix/eureka

Summary

In this chapter, we have learned how the domain-driven design model can be used in a µService. After running the demo application, we can see how each µService can be developed, deployed, and tested independently. You can create µServices using Spring Cloud very easily. We have also explored how one can use the Eureka registry and Discovery component with Spring Cloud.

In the next chapter, we will learn to deploy µServices in containers such as Docker. We will also understand µService testing using REST Java clients and other tools.

5
Deployment and Testing

This chapter will explain how to deploy microservices in different forms, from standalone to containers such as Docker. It will also demonstrate how Docker can be used to deploy our sample project on a cloud service such as AWS. Before implementing Docker, first we'll explore other factors about microservices, such as load balancing and Edge Server. You will also come to understand microservice testing using different REST clients such as RestTemplate, Netflix Feign, and so on.

In this chapter, we will cover the following topics:

- An overview of microservice architecture using Netflix OSS
- Load balancing microservices
- Edge Server
- Circuit breakers and monitoring
- Microservice deployment using containers
- Microservice integration testing using Docker containers

An overview of microservice architecture using Netflix OSS

Netflix are pioneers in microservice architecture. They were the first to successfully implement microservice architecture on a large scale. They also helped increase its popularity and contributed immensely to microservices by open sourcing most of their microservice tools with **Netflix Open Source Software Center (OSS)**.

According to the Netflix blog, when Netflix was developing their platform, they used Apache Cassandra for data storage, which is an open source tool from Apache. They started contributing to Cassandra with fixes and optimization extensions. This led to Netflix seeing the benefits of releasing Netflix projects with the name Open Source Software Center.

Spring took the opportunity to integrate many Netflix OSS projects, such as Zuul, Ribbon, Hystrix, Eureka Server, and Turbine, into Spring Cloud. This is one of the reasons Spring Cloud provides a ready-made platform for developing production-ready microservices. Now, let's take a look at a few important Netflix tools and how they fit into microservice architecture:

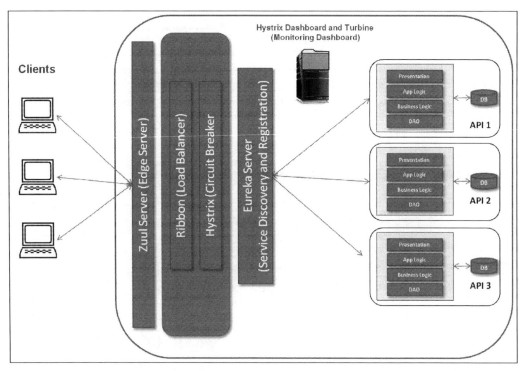

Microservice architecture diagram

As you can see in the preceding diagram, for each of the microservice practices, we have Netflix tool associated with it. We can go through the following mapping to understand it. Detailed information is covered in the respective sections of this chapter except concerning Eureka, which is elaborated on in the last chapter.

- **Edge Server**: We use Netflix Zuul Server as an Edge Server.
- **Load balancing**: Netflix Ribbon is used for load balancing.

- **Circuit breaker**: Netflix Hystrix is used as a circuit breaker and helps to keep the system up.

- **Service discovery and registration**: Netflix Eureka Server is used for service discovery and registration.

- **Monitoring dashboard**: Hystrix Dashboard is used with Netflix Turbine for microservice monitoring. It provides a dashboard to check the health of running microservices.

Load balancing

Load balancing is required to service requests in a manner that maximizes speed, capacity utilization, and it makes sure that no server is overloaded with requests. The load balancer also redirects requests to the remaining host servers if a server goes down. In microservice architecture, a microservice can serve internal or external requests. Based on this, we can have two types of load balancing – client-side and server-side load balancing.

Client-side load balancing

Microservices need interprocess communication so that services can communicate with each other. Spring Cloud uses Netflix Ribbon, a client-side load balancer that plays this critical role and can handle both HTTP and TCP. Ribbon is cloud-enabled and provides built-in failure resiliency. Ribbon also allows you to use multiple and pluggable load balancing rules. It integrates clients with load balancers.

In the last chapter, we added Eureka Server. Ribbon is integrated with Eureka Server in Spring Cloud by default. This integration provides the following features:

- You don't need to hardcode remote server URLs for discovery when Eureka Server is used. This is a prominent advantage, although you can still use the configured server list (*listOfServers*) in `application.yml` if required.

- The server list gets populated from Eureka Server. Eureka Server overrides `ribbonServerList` with `DiscoveryEnabledNIWSServerList`.

- The request to find out whether the server is up is delegated to Eureka. The `DiscoveryEnabledNIWSServerList` interface is used in place of Ribbon's `IPing`.

There are different clients available in Spring Cloud that use Ribbon, such as **RestTemplate** or **FeignClient**. These clients allow microservices to communicate with each other. Clients use instance IDs in place of hostnames and ports for making an HTTP call to service instances when Eureka Server is used. The client passes the service ID to Ribbon, Ribbon then uses the load balancer to pick the instance from the Eureka Server.

If there are multiple instances of services available in Eureka, as shown in the following screenshot, Ribbon picks only one for the request, based on load balancing algorithms:

Instances currently registered with Eureka

Application	AMIs	Availability Zones	Status
RESTAURANT-SERVICE	n/a (2)	(2)	**UP (2)** - SOUSHARM-IN:restaurant-service:5b034f31fd44c9ff6dd5c5fb1d4c83d7}, SOUSHARM-IN:restaurant-service:707b060d8d02e3516f3fde3c86c858d1}
ZUUL-SERVER	n/a (1)	(1)	**UP (1)** - SOUSHARM-IN:zuul-server:9094e5aae179efe903061d827e21e167}

Multiple service registration – Restaurant service

We can use `DiscoveryClient` to find all the available service instances in Eureka Server, as shown in the following code. Method `getLocalServiceInstance()` of class `DiscoveryClientSample` returns the all local service instances available in Eureka Server.

DiscoveryClient sample:

```
@Component
class DiscoveryClientSample implements CommandLineRunner {

    @Autowired
    private DiscoveryClient;

    @Override
    public void run(String... strings) throws Exception {
    //print the Discovery Client Description
        System.out.println(discoveryClient.description());
    // Get restaurant-service instances and prints its info
        discoveryClient.getInstances("restaurant-service").
forEach((ServiceInstance serviceInstance) -> {
            System.out.println(new StringBuilder("Instance -->
").append(serviceInstance.getServiceId())
```

```
                 .append("\nServer: ").append(serviceInstance.
getHost()).append(":").append(serviceInstance.getPort())
                 .append("\nURI: ").append(serviceInstance.
getUri()).append("\n\n\n"));
        });
    }
}
```

When executed, this code prints the following information. It shows two instances of
the Restaurant service:

```
Spring Cloud Eureka Discovery Client
Instance: RESTAURANT-SERVICE
Server: SOUSHARM-IN:3402
URI: http://SOUSHARM-IN:3402
Instance --> RESTAURANT-SERVICE
Server: SOUSHARM-IN:3368
URI: http://SOUSHARM-IN:3368
```

The following samples showcase how these clients can be used. You can see that
in both clients, the service name restaurant-service is used in place of a service
hostname and port. These clients call /v1/restaurants to get a list of restaurants
containing the name given in the name query parameter:

Rest Template sample:

```
@Override
public void run(String... strings) throws Exception {
ResponseEntity<Collection<Restaurant>> exchange
= this.restTemplate.exchange(
"http://restaurant-service/v1/restaurants?name=o",
                HttpMethod.GET,
                null,
                new ParameterizedTypeReference<Collection<Restaura
nt>>() {
                },
                ( "restaurants");
exchange.getBody().forEach((Restaurant restaurant) -> {
System.out.println(new StringBuilder("\n\n\n[ ").append(restaurant.
getId()).append(" ").append(restaurant.getName()).append("]"));
});
}
```

FeignClient sample:

```
@Component
class FeignSample implements CommandLineRunner {

    @Autowired
    private RestaurantClient restaurantClient;

    @Override
    public void run(String... strings) throws Exception {
        this.restaurantClient.getRestaurants("o").forEach((Restaurant
restaurant) -> {
            System.out.println(restaurant);
        });
    }
}


@FeignClient("restaurant-service")
interface RestaurantClient {

    @RequestMapping(method = RequestMethod.GET, value = "/v1/
restaurants")
    Collection<Restaurant> getRestaurants(@RequestParam("name") String
name);
}
```

All preceding examples will print the following output:

```
[ 1 Big-O Restaurant]
[ 2 O Restaurant]
```

Server-side load balancing

After client-side load balancing, it is important for us to define server-side load balancing. In addition, from the microservice architecture's point of view, it is important to define the routing mechanism for our OTRS app. For example, / may be mapped to our UI application, /restaurantapi is mapped to restaurant service, and /userapi is mapped to user service.

We'll use the Netflix Zuul Server as our Edge Server. Zuul is a JVM-based router and server-side load balancer. Zuul supports any JVM language for writing rules and filters and having the in-built support for Java and Groovy.

The external world (the UI and other clients) calls the Edge server, which uses the routes defined in `application.yml` to call internal services and provide the response. Your guess is right if you think it acts as a proxy server, carries gateway responsibility for internal networks, and calls internal services for defined and configured routes.

Normally, it is recommended to have a single Edge Server for all requests. However, few companies use a single Edge Server per client to scale. For example, Netflix uses a dedicated Edge Server for each device type.

An Edge Server will also be used in the next chapter, when we configure and implement microservice security.

Configuring and using the Edge Server is pretty simple in Spring Cloud. You need to use the following steps:

1. Define the Zuul Server dependency in `pom.xml`:

```
<dependency>
        <groupId>org.springframework.cloud</groupId>
        <artifactId>spring-cloud-starter-zuul</artifactId>
</dependency>
```

2. Use the `@EnableZuulProxy` annotation in your application class. It also internally uses `@EnableDiscoveryClient`: therefore it is also registered to Eureka Server automatically. You can find the registered Zuul Server in the last figure: *Multiple service registration – Restaurant service*".

3. Update the Zuul configuration in `application.yml`, as the following shows:

   ○ `zuul:ignoredServices`: This skips the automatic addition of services. We can define service ID patterns here. * denotes that we are ignoring all services. In the following sample, all services are ignored except `restaurant-service`.

   ○ `Zuul.routes`: This contains the `path` attribute that defines the URI's pattern. Here, `/restaurantapi` is mapped to Restaurant Service using `serviceId`. `serviceId` represents the service in Eureka Server. You can use a URL in place of a service, if Eureka Server is not used. We have also used the `stripPrefix` attribute to strip the prefix (`/restaurantapi`), and the resultant `/restaurantapi/v1/restaurants/1` call converts to `/v1/restaurants/1` while calling the service:

   application.yml
   ```
   info:
       component: Zuul Server
   ```

```
# Spring properties
spring:
  application:
    name: zuul-server  # Service registers under this name

endpoints:
    restart:
        enabled: true
    shutdown:
        enabled: true
    health:
        sensitive: false

zuul:
    ignoredServices: "*"
    routes:
        restaurantapi:
            path: / restaurantapi/**
            serviceId: restaurant-service
            stripPrefix: true

server:
    port: 8765

# Discovery Server Access
eureka:
  instance:
    leaseRenewalIntervalInSeconds: 3
    metadataMap:
      instanceId: ${vcap.application.instance_id:${spring.
application.name}:${spring.application.instance_id:${random.
value}}}
    serviceUrl:
      defaultZone: http://localhost:8761/eureka/
    fetchRegistry: false
```

Let's see a working Edge Server. First, we'll call the restaurant service deployed on port 3402, shown as follows:

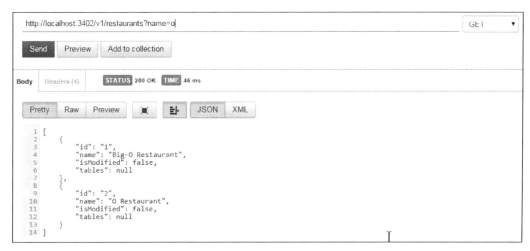

Direct Restaurant service call

Then, we'll call the same service using the Edge Server that is deployed on port 8765. You can see that the /restaurantapi prefix is used for calling /v1/restaurants?name=o, and it gives the same result:

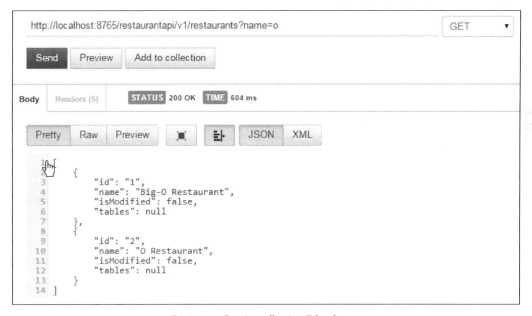

Restaurant Service call using Edge Server

Circuit breaker and monitoring

In general terms, a circuit breaker is:

An automatic device for stopping the flow of current in an electric circuit as a safety measure.

The same concept is used for microservice development, known as the Circuit Breaker design pattern. It tracks the availability of external services such as Eureka Server, API services such as `restaurant-service`, and so on, and prevents service consumers from performing any action on any service that is not available.

It is another important aspect of microservice architecture, a safety measure (failsafe mechanism) when the service does not respond to a call made by the service consumer – circuit breaker.

We'll use Netflix Hystrix as a circuit breaker. It calls the internal fallback method in the service consumer when failures occur (for example due to a communication error or timeout). It executes embedded within its consumer of service. In the next section, you will find the code that implements this feature.

Hystrix opens the circuit and fail-fast when the service fails to respond repeatedly, until the service is available again. You must be wondering, if Hystrix opens the circuit, then how does it know that the service is available? It exceptionally allows some requests to call the service.

Using Hystrix's fallback methods

There are three steps for implementing fallback methods:

1. **Enable the circuit breaker**: The main class of microservice that consumes other services should be annotated with `@EnableCircuitBreaker`. For example, if a user service would like to get the restaurant details, where a user has reserved the table:

   ```
   @SpringBootApplication
   @EnableCircuitBreaker
   @ComponentScan({"com.packtpub.mmj.user.service", "com.packtpub.
   mmj.common"})
   public class UsersApp {
   ```

2. **Configure the fallback method**: To configure the `fallbackMethod`, the `@HystrixCommand` annotation is used:

```
@HystrixCommand(fallbackMethod = "defaultRestaurant")
public ResponseEntity<Restaurant> getRestaurantById(int
restaurantId) {

    LOG.debug("Get Restaurant By Id with Hystrix protection");

    URI uri = util.getServiceUrl("restaurant-service");

    String url = uri.toString() + "/v1/restaurants/" +
restaurantId;
    LOG.debug("Get Restaurant By Id URL: {}", url);

    ResponseEntity<Restaurant> response = restTemplate.
getForEntity(url, Restaurant.class);
    LOG.debug("Get Restaurant By Id http-status: {}", response.
getStatusCode());
    LOG.debug("GET Restaurant body: {}", response.getBody());

    Restaurant restaurant = response.getBody();
    LOG.debug("Restaurant ID: {}", restaurant.getId());

    return serviceHelper.createOkResponse(restaurant);
}
```

3. **Define fallback method**: A method that handles the failure and performs the steps for safety:

```
public ResponseEntity<Restaurant> defaultRestaurant(int
restaurantId) {
    LOG.warn("Fallback method for restaurant-service is being
used.");
    return serviceHelper.createResponse(null, HttpStatus.BAD_
GATEWAY);
}
```

These steps should be enough to failsafe the service calls and return a more appropriate response to the service consumer.

Monitoring

Hystrix provides the dashboard with a web UI that provides nice graphics of circuit breakers:

Default Hystrix dashboard

Netflix Turbine is a web application that connects to the instances of your Hystrix applications in a cluster and aggregates information, which it does in real time (updated every 0.5 seconds). Turbine provides information using a stream that is known as a turbine stream.

If you combine Hystrix with Netflix Turbine, then you can get all the information from Eureka Server on the Hystrix dashboard. This gives you a landscape view of all the information about the circuit breakers.

To use Turbine with Hystrix, just type in the Turbine URL `http://localhost:8989/turbine.stream` (port `8989` is configured for the Turbine server in `application.yml`) in first textbox shown before, and click on **Monitory Stream**.

Netflix Hystrix and Turbine uses RabbitMQ, an open source message queuing software. RabbitMQ works on **Advance Messaging Queue Protocol (AMQP)**. It is a software in which queues can be defined, where applications can establish a connection and transfer a message through it. A message can include any kind of information. A message can be stored in the RabbitMQ queue until a receiver application connects and receives the message (taking the message off the queue).

Hystrix uses RabbitMQ to send a metrics data feed to Turbine.

 Before we configure Hystrix and Turbine, please install the RabbitMQ application on your platform. Hystrix and Turbine use RabbitMQ to communicate between themselves.

Setting up the Hystrix Dashboard

We'll add the new Maven dependency, `dashboard-server` for Hystrix Server. Configuring and using the Hystrix Dashboard is pretty simple in Spring Cloud like others. You just need to follow these steps:

1. Define the Hystrix Dashboard dependency in `pom.xml`:

```
<dependency>
        <groupId>org.springframework.cloud</groupId>
        <artifactId>spring-cloud-starter- hystrix-dashboard</
artifactId>
</dependency>
```

2. The `@EnableHystrixDashboard` annotation in the main Java class does everything for you to use it. We'll also use the `@Controller` to forward the request from the root to Hystrix, as shown here:

```
@SpringBootApplication
@Controller
@EnableHystrixDashboard
public class DashboardApp extends SpringBootServletInitializer {

    @RequestMapping("/")
    public String home() {
        return "forward:/hystrix";
    }

    @Override
    protected SpringApplicationBuilder configure(SpringApplication
Builder application) {
```

```
            return application.sources(DashboardApp.class).web(true);
    }

    public static void main(String[] args) {
        SpringApplication.run(DashboardApp.class, args);
    }
}
```

3. Update the Dashboard application configuration in `application.yml`, as shown here:

```
application.yml
# Hystrix Dashboard properties
spring:
    application:
        name: dashboard-server

endpoints:
    restart:
        enabled: true
    shutdown:
        enabled: true

server:
    port: 7979

eureka:
    instance:
        leaseRenewalIntervalInSeconds: 3
        metadataMap:
            instanceId: ${vcap.application.instance_id:${spring.
application.name}:${spring.application.instance_id:${random.
value}}}

    client:
        # Default values comes from org.springframework.cloud.
netflix.eurek.EurekaClientConfigBean
        registryFetchIntervalSeconds: 5
        instanceInfoReplicationIntervalSeconds: 5
        initialInstanceInfoReplicationIntervalSeconds: 5
        serviceUrl:
            defaultZone: http://localhost:8761/eureka/
        fetchRegistry: false

logging:
```

```
level:
    ROOT: WARN
    org.springframework.web: WARN
```

Setting up Turbine

We'll create one more Maven dependency for Turbine. When you run the Hystrix Dashboard application, it will look like the *Default Hystrix Dashboard* screenshot shown earlier.

Now, we will configure the Turbine Server using the following steps:

1. Define the Turbine Server dependency in pom.xml:

```
<dependency>
    <groupId>org.springframework.cloud</groupId>
    <artifactId>spring-cloud-starter-turbine-amqp</artifactId>
</dependency>
```

2. Use the @EnableTurbineAmqp annotation in your application class as shown here. We are also defining a bean that will return the RabbitMQ Connection Factory:

```
@SpringBootApplication
@EnableTurbineAmqp
@EnableDiscoveryClient
public class TurbineApp {

    private static final Logger LOG = LoggerFactory.
getLogger(TurbineApp.class);

    @Value("${app.rabbitmq.host:localhost}")
    String rabbitMQHost;

    @Bean
    public ConnectionFactory connectionFactory() {
        LOG.info("Creating RabbitMQHost ConnectionFactory for
host: {}", rabbitMQHost);
        CachingConnectionFactory cachingConnectionFactory = new Ca
chingConnectionFactory(rabbitMQHost);
        return cachingConnectionFactory;
    }

    public static void main(String[] args) {
        SpringApplication.run(TurbineApp.class, args);
    }
}
```

3. Update the Turbine configuration in `application.yml`, as shown here:

`server:port`: The main port used by the the turbine HTTP

`management:port`: Port of turbine Actuator endpoints

```
application.yml
spring:
    application:
        name: turbine-server

server:
    port: 8989

management:
    port: 8990

PREFIX:

endpoints:
    restart:
        enabled: true
    shutdown:
        enabled: true

eureka:
    instance:
        leaseRenewalIntervalInSeconds: 10
    client:
        registryFetchIntervalSeconds: 5
        instanceInfoReplicationIntervalSeconds: 5
        initialInstanceInfoReplicationIntervalSeconds: 5
        serviceUrl:
            defaultZone: http://localhost:8761/eureka/

logging:
    level:
        root: WARN
        com.netflix.discovery: 'OFF'
```

 Please be aware the preceding steps always create the respective servers with default configurations. If required, you can override the default configuration with specific settings.

Microservice deployment using containers

You might have got the point about Docker after reading *Chapter 1*, *A Solution Approach*.

A Docker container provides a lightweight runtime environment, consisting of the core features of a virtual machine and the isolated services of operating systems, known as a docker image. Docker makes the packaging and execution of μServices easier and smoother. Each operating system can have multiple Dockers, and each Docker can run multiple applications.

Installation and configuration

Docker needs a virtualized server if you are not using a Linux OS. You can install VirtualBox or similar tools such as Docker Toolbox to make it work for you. The Docker installation page gives more details about it and lets you know how to do it. So, leave it to the Docker installation guide available on Docker's website.

You can install Docker, based on your platform, by following the instructions given at `https://docs.docker.com/engine/installation/`.

DockerToolbox-1.9.1f was the latest version available at the time of writing. This is the version we used.

Docker Machine with 4 GB

Default machines are created with 2 GB of memory. We'll recreate a Docker Machine with 4 GB of memory:

```
docker-machine rm default
docker-machine create -d virtualbox --virtualbox-memory 4096 default
```

Building Docker images with Maven

There are various Docker maven plugins that can be used:

* `https://github.com/rhuss/docker-maven-plugin`
* `https://github.com/alexec/docker-maven-plugin`
* `https://github.com/spotify/docker-maven-plugin`

You can use any of these, based on your choice. I found the Docker Maven plugin by `@rhuss` to be best suited for us. It is updated regularly and has many extra features when compared to the others.

We need to introduce the Docker Spring Profile in `application.yml` before we start discussing the configuration of `docker-maven-plugin`. It will make our job easier when building services for various platforms. We need to configure the following four properties:

- We'll use the Spring profile identified as Docker.
- There won't be any conflict of ports among embedded Tomcat, since services will be executed in their own respective containers. We can now use port `8080`.
- We will prefer to use an IP address to register our services in Eureka. Therefore, the Eureka instance property `preferIpAddress` will be set to `true`.
- Finally, we'll use the Eureka Server host name in `serviceUrl:defaultZone`.

To add a Spring profile in your project, add the following lines in `application.yml` after the existing content:

```
---
# For deployment in Docker containers
spring:
  profiles: docker

server:
  port: 8080

eureka:
  instance:
    preferIpAddress: true
  client:
    serviceUrl:
      defaultZone: http://eureka:8761/eureka/
```

We will also add the following code in `pom.xml` to activate the Spring profile Docker, while building a Docker container JAR. (This will create the JAR using the previously defined properties, for example `port:8080`.)

```
<profiles>
    <profile>
        <id>docker</id>
        <properties>
            <spring.profiles.active>docker</spring.profiles.active>
        </properties>
    </profile>
</profiles>
```

We just need to use Maven `docker` profile while building the service, shown as follows:

```
mvn -P docker clean package
```

The preceding command will generate the `service` JAR with Tomcat's 8080 port and will get registered on Eureka Server with the hostname `eureka`.

Now, let's configure `docker-maven-plugin` to build the image with our restaurant microservice. This plugin has to create a Dockerfile first. The Dockerfile is configured in two places – in `pom.xml` and `docker-assembly.xml`. We'll use the following plugin configuration in `pom.xml`:

```
<properties>
<!-- For Docker hub leave empty; use "localhost:5000/" for a local
Docker Registry -->
  <docker.registry.name>localhost:5000/</docker.registry.name>
  <docker.repository.name>${docker.registry.name}sourabhh /${project.
artifactId}</docker.repository.name>
</properties>
...
<plugin>
  <groupId>org.jolokia</groupId>
  <artifactId>docker-maven-plugin</artifactId>
  <version>0.13.7</version>
  <configuration>
    <images>
      <image>
<name>${docker.repository.name}:${project.version}</name>
        <alias>${project.artifactId}</alias>

      <build>
        <from>java:8-jre</from>
        <maintainer>sourabhh</maintainer>
        <assembly>
          <descriptor>docker-assembly.xml</descriptor>
        </assembly>
        <ports>
          <port>8080</port>
        </ports>
        <cmd>
          <shell>java -jar \
            /maven/${project.build.finalName}.jar server \
            /maven/docker-config.yml</shell>
        </cmd>
      </build>
```

```
        <run>
        <!-- To Do -->
        </run>
      </image>
    </images>
  </configuration>
</plugin>
```

Above the Docker Maven plugin configuration, create a Dockerfile that creates the JRE 8 (java:8-jre) -based image. This exposes ports 8080 and 8081.

Next, we'll configure docker-assembly.xml, which tells the plugin which files should be put into the container. It will be placed under src/main/docker:

```
<assembly xmlns="http://maven.apache.org/plugins/maven-assembly-
plugin/assembly/1.1.2" xmlns:xsi="http://www.w3.org/2001/XMLSchema-
instance"
   xsi:schemaLocation="http://maven.apache.org/plugins/maven-assembly-
plugin/assembly/1.1.2 http://maven.apache.org/xsd/assembly-1.1.2.xsd">
  <id>${project.artifactId}</id>
  <files>
    <file>
      <source>{basedir}/target/${project.build.finalName}.jar</source>
      <outputDirectory>/</outputDirectory>
    </file>
    <file>
      <source>src/main/resources/docker-config.yml</source>
      <outputDirectory>/</outputDirectory>
    </file>
  </files>
</assembly>
```

Above assembly, add the service JAR and docker-config.yml in the generated Dockerfile. This Dockerfile is located under target/docker/. On opening this file, you will find the content to be similar to this:

```
FROM java:8-jre
MAINTAINER sourabhh
EXPOSE 8080
COPY maven /maven/
CMD java -jar \
  /maven/restaurant-service.jar server \
  /maven/docker-config.yml
```

The preceding file can be found at `restaurant-service\target\docker\sousharm\` `restaurant-service\PACKT-SNAPSHOT\build`. The `build` directory also contains the `maven` directory, which contains everything mentioned in `docker-assembly.xml`.

Lets' build the Docker Image:

```
mvn docker:build
```

Once this command completes, we can validate the image in the local repository using Docker Images, or by running the following command:

```
docker run -it -p 8080:8080 sourabhh/restaurant-service:PACKT-SNAPSHOT
```

Use `-it` to execute this command in the foreground, in place of `-d`.

Running Docker using Maven

To execute a Docker Image with Maven, we need to add the following configuration in the `pom.xml`. `<run>` block, to be put where we marked the *To Do* under the image block of `docker-maven-plugin` section in the `pom.xml` file:

```
<properties>
  <docker.host.address>localhost</docker.host.address>
  <docker.port>8080</docker.port>
</properties>
...
<run>
  <namingStrategy>alias</namingStrategy>
  <ports>
    <port>${docker.port}:8080</port>
  </ports>
  <volumes>
    <bind>
      <volume>${user.home}/logs:/logs</volume>
    </bind>
  </volumes>
  <wait>
    <url>http://${docker.host.address}:${docker.port}/v1/
restaurants/1</url>
    <time>100000</time>
  </wait>
  <log>
    <prefix>${project.artifactId}</prefix>
    <color>cyan</color>
  </log>
</run>
```

Here, we have defined the parameters for running our Restaurant service container. We have mapped Docker container ports `8080` and `8081` to the host system's ports, which allows us to access the service. Similarly, we have also bound the containers' logs directory to the host systems' `<home>/logs` directory.

The Docker Maven plugin can detect if the container has finished starting up by polling the ping URL of the admin backend until it receives an answer.

Please note that Docker host is not *localhost* if you are using DockerToolbox or boot2docker on Windows or Mac OS X. You can check the Docker Image IP by executing `docker-machine ip default`. It is also shown while starting up.

The Docker container is ready to start. Use the following command to start it using Maven:

```
mvn docker:start .
```

Integration testing with Docker

Starting and stopping a Docker container can be done by binding the following executions to the `docker-maven-plugin` life cycle phase in `pom.xml`:

```
<execution>
  <id>start</id>
  <phase>pre-integration-test</phase>
  <goals>
    <goal>build</goal>
    <goal>start</goal>
  </goals>
</execution>
<execution>
  <id>stop</id>
  <phase>post-integration-test</phase>
  <goals>
    <goal>stop</goal>
  </goals>
</execution>
```

We will now configure the failsafe plugin to perform integration testing with Docker. This allows us to execute the integration tests. We are passing the service URL in the `service.url` tag, so that our integration test can use it to perform integration testing.

We'll use the `DockerIntegrationTest` marker to mark our Docker integration tests. It is defined as follows:

```
package com.packtpub.mmj.restaurant.resources.docker;

public interface DockerIntegrationTest {
    // Marker for Docker integratino Tests
}
```

Look at the following integration plugin code. You can see that `DockerIntegrationTest` is configured for the inclusion of integration tests (failsafe plugin), whereas it is used for excluding in unit tests (Surefire plugin):

```
<plugin>
  <groupId>org.apache.maven.plugins</groupId>
  <artifactId>maven-failsafe-plugin</artifactId>
  <version>2.18.1</version>
  <configuration>
    <phase>integration-test</phase>
    <includes>
      <include>**/*.java</include>
    </includes>
    <groups>com.packtpub.mmj.restaurant.resources.docker.
DockerIntegrationTest</groups>
    <systemPropertyVariables>
      <service.url>http://${docker.host.address}:${docker.port}/</
service.url>
    </systemPropertyVariables>
  </configuration>
  <executions>
    <execution>
      <goals>
        <goal>integration-test</goal>
      </goals>
    </execution>
  </executions>
</plugin>
<plugin>
  <groupId>org.apache.maven.plugins</groupId>
  <artifactId>maven-surefire-plugin</artifactId>
  <version>2.18.1</version>
  <configuration>
    <excludedGroups>com.packtpub.mmj.restaurant.resources.docker.
DockerIntegrationTest</excludedGroups>
  </configuration>
</plugin>
```

A simple integration test looks like this:

```
@Category(DockerIntegrationTest.class)
public class RestaurantAppDockerIT {

    @Test
    public void testConnection() throws IOException {
        String baseUrl = System.getProperty("service.url");
        URL serviceUrl = new URL(baseUrl + "v1/restaurants/1");
        HttpURLConnection connection = (HttpURLConnection) serviceUrl.
openConnection();
        int responseCode = connection.getResponseCode();
        assertEquals(200, responseCode);
    }
}
```

You can use the following command to perform integration testing using Maven:

```
mvn integration-test
```

Pushing the image to a registry

Add the following tags under `docker-maven-plugin` to publish the Docker Image to Docker Hub:

```
<execution>
  <id>push-to-docker-registry</id>
  <phase>deploy</phase>
  <goals>
    <goal>push</goal>
  </goals>
</execution>
```

You can skip JAR publishing by using the following configuration for `maven-deploy-plugin`:

```
<plugin>
  <groupId>org.apache.maven.plugins</groupId>
  <artifactId>maven-deploy-plugin</artifactId>
  <version>2.7</version>
  <configuration>
    <skip>true</skip>
  </configuration>
</plugin>
```

Publishing a Docker image in Docker Hub also requires a username and password:

```
mvn -Ddocker.username=<username> -Ddocker.password=<password> deploy
```

You can also push a Docker image to your own Docker registry. To do this, add the `docker.registry.name` tag as shown in the following code. For example, if your Docker registry is available at `xyz.domain.com` on port `4994`, then define it by adding the following line of code:

```
<docker.registry.name>xyz.domain.com: 4994</docker.reqistry.name>
```

This does the job and we can not only deploy, but also test our Dockerized service.

Managing Docker containers

Each microservice will have its own Docker container. Therefore, we'll use the *Docker Compose* Docker container manager to manage our containers.

Docker Compose will help us to specify the number of containers and how these will be executed. We can specify the Docker Image, ports, and each container's links to other Docker containers.

We'll create a file called `docker-compose.yml` in our root project directory and add all the microservice containers to it. We'll first specify the Eureka Server as follows:

```
eureka:
  image: localhost:5000/sourabhh/eureka-server
  ports:
    - "8761:8761"
```

Here, image represents the published Docker image for Eureka Server and ports represents the mapping between the host being used for executing the Docker Image and the Docker host.

This will start Eureka Server and publish the specified ports for external access.

Now, our services can use these containers (dependent containers such as Eureka). Let's see how `restaurant-service` can be linked to dependent containers. It is simple; just use the `links` directive:

```
restaurant-service:
  image: localhost:5000/sourabhh/restaurant-service
  ports:
    - "8080:8080"
  links:
    - eureka
```

The preceding links declaration will update the /etc/hosts file in the restaurant-service container with one line per service that the restaurant-service depends on (let's assume the security container is also linked), for example:

```
192.168.0.22  security
192.168.0.31  eureka
```

If you don't have a docker local registry set up, then please do this first for issue-less or smoother execution.

Build the docker local registry by:

```
docker run -d -p 5000:5000 --restart=always --name
registry registry:2
```

Then, perform push and pull commands for the local images:

```
docker push localhost:5000/sourabhh/restaurant-
service:PACKT-SNAPSHOT
docker-compose pull
```

Finally, execute docker-compose:

```
docker-compose up -d
```

Once all the microservice containers (service and server) are configured, we can start all Docker containers with a single command:

```
docker-compose up -d
```

This will start up all Docker containers configured in Docker Composer. The following command will list them:

```
docker-compose ps
```

```
Name                                             Command

                   State          Ports
----------------------------------------------------------------
onlinetablereservation5_eureka_1          /bin/sh -c java -jar        ...
Up       0.0.0.0:8761->8761/tcp


onlinetablereservation5_restaurant-service_1   /bin/sh -c java -jar
...    Up       0.0.0.0:8080->8080/tcp
```

You can also check docker image logs using the following command:

```
docker-compose logs
```

```
[36mrestaurant-service_1 | ←[0m2015-12-23 08:20:46.819  INFO 7 --- [pool-
3-thread-1] com.netflix.discovery.DiscoveryClient    : DiscoveryClient_
RESTAURANT-SERVICE/172.17
```

```
0.4:restaurant-service:93d93a7bd1768dcb3d86c858e520d3ce - Re-registering
apps/RESTAURANT-SERVICE

[36mrestaurant-service_1 | ←[0m2015-12-23 08:20:46.820  INFO 7 --- [pool-
3-thread-1] com.netflix.discovery.DiscoveryClient    : DiscoveryClient_
RESTAURANT-SERVICE/172.17

0.4:restaurant-service:93d93a7bd1768dcb3d86c858e520d3ce: registering
service...

[36mrestaurant-service_1 | ←[0m2015-12-23 08:20:46.917  INFO 7 --- [pool-
3-thread-1] com.netflix.discovery.DiscoveryClient    : DiscoveryClient_
RESTAURANT-SERVICE/172.17
```

References

The following links will give you more information:

- **Netflix Ribbon**: https://github.com/Netflix/ribbon
- **Netflix Zuul**: https://github.com/Netflix/zuul
- **RabbitMQ**: https://www.rabbitmq.com/download.html
- **Hystrix**: https://github.com/Netflix/Hystrix
- **Turbine**: https://github.com/Netflix/Turbine
- **Docker**: https://www.docker.com/

Summary

In this chapter, we have learned about various microservice management features: – load balancing, Edge Server (Gateway), circuit breakers, and monitoring. You should now know how to implement load balancing and routing after going through this chapter. We have also learned how Edge Server can be set up and configured. The failsafe mechanism is another important part that you have learned in this chapter. Deployment can be made simple by using Docker or any other container. Docker was demonstrated and integrated using Maven Build.

From a testing point of view, we performed the integration testing on the Docker image of the service. We also explored the way we can write clients such as RestTemplate and Netflix Feign.

In the next chapter, we will learn to secure the μServices with respect to authentication and authorization. We will also explore the other aspects of microservice securities.

6
Securing Microservices

As you know, microservices are the components that we deploy in on-premises or cloud infrastructure. Microservices may offer APIs or web applications. Our sample application, OTRS, offers APIs. This chapter will focus on how to secure these APIs using Spring Security and Spring OAuth2. We'll also focus on OAuth 2.0 fundamentals. We'll use OAuth 2.0 to secure the OTRS APIs. For more understanding on securing REST APIs, you can refer to *RESTful Java Web Services Security*, *Packt Publishing* book. You can also refer to *Spring Security [Video]*, *Packt Publishing* video, for more information on Spring Security. We'll also learn about Cross Origin Request Site filters, and cross-site scripting blockers.

In this chapter, we will cover the following topics:

- Enabling Secure Socket Layer (SSL)
- Authentication and authorization
- OAuth 2.0

Enabling Secure Socket Layer

So far, we are using the **Hyper Text Transfer Protocol** (**HTTP**). HTTP transfers data in plain text, but data transfer over the Internet in plain text is not a good idea at all. It makes hackers' jobs easy and allows them to get your private information, such as your user ID, passwords, and credit card details easily using a packet sniffer.

We definitely don't want to compromise user data, so we will provide the most secure way to access our web application. Therefore, we need to encrypt the information that is exchanged between the end user and our application. We'll use **Secure Socket Layer (SSL)** or **Transport Security Layer (TSL)** to encrypt the data.

SSL is a protocol designed to provide security (encryption) for network communications. HTTP associates with SSL to provide the secure implementation of HTTP, known as **Hyper Text Transfer Protocol Secure**, or **Hyper Text Transfer Protocol over SSL (HTTPS)**. HTTPS makes sure that the privacy and integrity of the exchanged data is protected. It also ensures the authenticity of websites visited. This security centers around the distribution of signed digital certificates between the server hosting the application, the end user's machine, and a third-party trust store server. Let's see how this process takes place:

1. The end user sends the request to the web application, for example `http://twitter.com`, using a web browser.

2. On receiving the request, the server redirects the browser to `https://twitter.com` using the HTTP code 302.

3. The end user's browser connects to `https://twitter.com` and, in response, the server provides the certificate containing the digital signature to the end user's browser.

4. The end user's browser receives this certificate and sends it to a trusted **Certificate Authority (CA)** for verification.

5. Once the certificate gets verified all the way to the root CA, an encrypted communication is established between the end user's browser and the application hosting server.

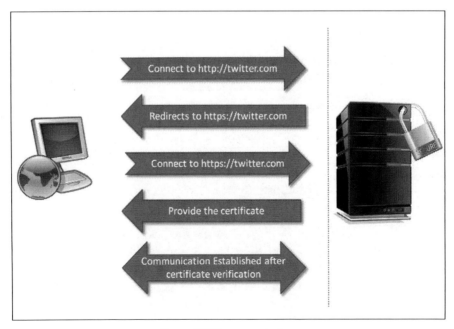

Secure HTTP communication

Although SSL ensures security in terms of encryption and web application authenticity, it does not safeguard against phishing and other attacks. Professional hackers can decrypt information sent using HTTPS.

Now, after going over the basics of SSL, let's implement it for our sample OTRS project. We don't need to implement SSL for all microservices. All microservices will be accessed using our proxy or edge server; Zuul-server by the external environment, except our new microservice, security-service, which we will introduce in this chapter for authentication and authorization.

First, we'll set up SSL in edge server. We need to have the keystore that is required for enabling SSL in embedded Tomcat. We'll use the self-signed certificate for demonstration. We'll use Java keytool to generate the keystore using the following command. You can use any other tool also:

```
keytool -genkey -keyalg RSA -alias selfsigned -keystore keystore.jks -ext
san=dns:localhost -storepass password -validity 365 -keysize 2048
```

It asks for information such as name, address details, organization, and so on (see the following screenshot):

```
C:\dev\workspace\ms\online-table-reservation-6>keytool -genkey -keyalg RSA -alias selfsigned -keystor
what is your first and last name?
  [Unknown]:  localhost
what is the name of your organizational unit?
  [Unknown]:  org unit
what is the name of your organization?
  [Unknown]:  org
what is the name of your City or Locality?
  [Unknown]:  city
what is the name of your State or Province?
  [Unknown]:  state
what is the two-letter country code for this unit?
  [Unknown]:  CN
Is CN=localhost, OU=org unit, O=org, L=city, ST=state, C=CN correct?
  [no]:  yes

Enter key password for <selfsigned>
        (RETURN if same as keystore password):
Re-enter new password:

C:\dev\workspace\ms\online-table-reservation-6>
```

The keytool generates keys

Be aware of the following points to ensure the proper functioning of self-signed certificates:

- Use `-ext` to define **Subject Alternative Names (SAN)**. You can also use IP (for example, `san=ip:190.19.0.11`). Earlier, use of the hostname of the machine, where application deployment takes place was being used as most **common name (CN)**. It prevents the `java.security.cert.CertificateException` for `No name matching localhost found`.

- You can use a browser or OpenSSL to download the certificate. Add the newly generated certificate to the cacerts keystore located at `jre/lib/security/cacerts` inside active `JDK/JRE` home directory by using the `keytool -importcert` command. Note that `changeit` is the default password for the cacerts keystore. Run the following command:

```
keytool -importcert -file path/to/.crt -alias <cert alias>
-keystore <JRE/JAVA_HOME>/jre/lib/security/cacerts -storepass
changeit
```

> Self-signed certificates can be used only for development and testing purposes. The use of these certificates in a production environment does not provide the required security. Always use the certificates provided and signed by trusted signing authorities in production environments. Store your private keys safely.

Now, after putting the generated `keystore.jks` in the `src/main/resources` directory of the OTRS project, along with `application.yml`, we can update this information in EdgeServer `application.yml` as follows:

```
server:
    ssl:
        key-store: classpath:keystore.jks
        key-store-password: password
        key-password: password
    port: 8765
```

Rebuild the Zuul-server JAR to use the HTTPS.

> The key store file can be stored in the preceding class path in Tomcat version 7.0.66+ and 8.0.28+. For older versions, you can use the path of the key store file for the `server:ssl:key-store` value.

Similarly, you can configure SSL for other microservices.

Authentication and authorization

Providing authentication and authorization is de facto for web applications. We'll discuss authentication and authorization in this section. The new paradigm that has evolved over the past few years is OAuth. We'll learn and use OAuth 2.0 for implementation. OAuth is an open authorization mechanism, implemented in every major web application. Web applications can access each other's data by implementing the OAuth standard. It has become the most popular way to authenticate oneself for various web applications. Like on www.quora.com, you can register, and login using your Google or Twitter login IDs. It is also more user friendly, as client applications (for example, www.quora.com) don't need to store the user's passwords. The end user does not need to remember one more user ID and password.

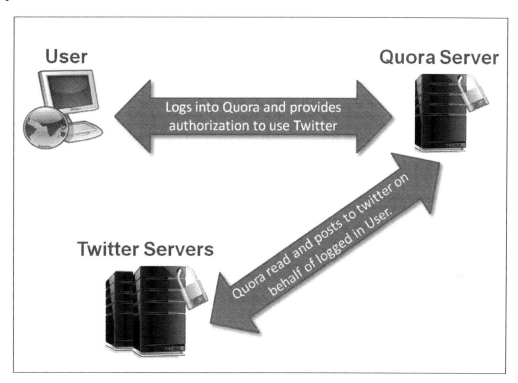

OAuth 2.0 example usage

OAuth 2.0

The **Internet Engineering Task Force (IETF)** governs the standards and specifications of OAuth. OAuth 1.0a was the most recent version before OAuth 2.0 that was having a fix for session-fixation security flaw in the OAuth 1.0. OAuth 1.0 and 1.0a were very different from OAuth 2.0. OAuth 1.0 relies on security certificates and channel binding. OAuth 2.0 does not support security certification and channel binding. It works completely on **Transport Security Layer (TSL)**. Therefore, OAuth 2.0 does not provide backward compatibility.

Usage of OAuth

- As discussed, it can be used for authentication. You might have seen it in various applications, displaying messages such as sign in using Facebook or sign in using Twitter.

- Applications can use it to read data from other applications, such as by integrating a Facebook widget into the application, or having a Twitter feed on your blog.

- Or, the opposite of the previous point can be true: you enable other applications to access the end user's data.

OAuth 2.0 specification – concise details

We'll try to discuss and understand the OAuth 2.0 specifications in a concise manner. Let's first see how signing in using Twitter works.

Please note that the process mentioned here was used at the time of writing. It may change in future. However, this process describes one of the OAuth 2.0 processes properly:

1. The user visits the Quora home page. It shows various login options. We'll explore the process of the **Continue with Twitter** link.

2. When the user clicks on the **Continue with Twitter** link, Quora opens a new window (in Chrome) that redirects the user to the www.twitter.com application. During this process few web applications redirect the user to the same opened tab/window.

3. In this new window/tab, the user signs in to www.twitter.com with their credentials.

4. If the user has not authorized the Quora application to use their data earlier, Twitter asks for the user's permission to authorize Quora to access the user's information. If the user has already authorized Quora, then this step is skipped.

5. After proper authentication, Twitter redirects the user to Quora's redirect URI with an authentication code.

6. Quora sends the client ID, client secret token, and authentication code (sent by Twitter in step 5) to Twitter when Quora redirect URI entered in the browser.

7. After validating these parameters, Twitter sends the access token to Quora.

8. The user is logged in to Quora on successful retrieval of the access token.

9. Quora may use this access token to retrieve user information from Quora.

You must be wondering how Twitter got Quora's redirect URI, client ID, and secret token. Quora works as a client application and Twitter as an authorization server. Quora, as a client, registered on Twitter by using Twitter's OAuth implementation to use resource owner (end user) information. Quora provides a redirect URI at the time of registration. Twitter provides the client ID and secret token to Quora. It works this way. In OAuth 2.0, user information is known as user resources. Twitter provides a resource server and an authorization server. We'll discuss more of these OAuth terms in the next sections.

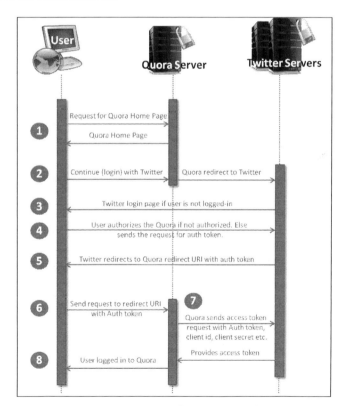

OAuth 2.0 example process for signing in with Twitter

OAuth 2.0 roles

There are four roles defined in the OAuth 2.0 specifications:

- Resource owner
- Resource server
- Client
- Authorization server

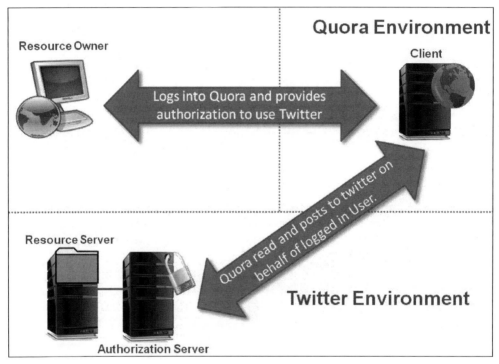

OAuth 2.0 roles

Resource owner

For the Quora sign in using Twitter example, the Twitter user was the resource owner. The resource owner is an entity that owns the protected resources (for example user handle, tweets and so on) that are to be shared. This entity can be an application or a person. We call this entity the resource owner because it can only grant access to its resources. Specification also defines, when resource owner is a person, it is referred to as an end user.

Resource server

The resource server hosts the protected resources. It should be capable of serving the access requests to these resources using access tokens. For the Quora sign in using Twitter example, Twitter is the resource server.

Client

For the Quora sign in using Twitter example, Quora is the client. The client is the application that makes access requests for protected resources to the resource server on behalf of the resource owner.

Authorization server

The authorization server provides different tokens to the client application, such as access tokens or refresh tokens, only after the resource owner authenticates themselves.

OAuth 2.0 does not provide any specifications for interactions between the resource server and the authorization server. Therefore, the authorization server and resource server can be on the same server, or can be on a separate one.

A single authorization server can also be used to issue access tokens for multiple resource servers.

OAuth 2.0 client registration

The client that communicates with the authorization server to obtain the access key for a resource should first be registered with the authorization server. The OAuth 2.0 specification does not specify the way a client registers with the authorization server. Registration does not require direct communication between the client and the authorization server. Registration can be done using self-issued or third-party-issued assertions. The authorization server obtains the required client properties using one of these assertions. Let's see what the client properties are:

- Client type (discussed in the next section).
- Client redirect URI, as we discussed in the Quora sign in using Twitter example. This is one of the endpoints used for OAuth 2.0. We will discuss other endpoints in the *Endpoints* section.
- Any other information required by the authorization server, for example client name, description, logo image, contact details, acceptance of legal terms and conditions, and so on.

Client types

There are two types of client described by the specification, based on their ability to maintain the confidentiality of client credentials: confidential and public. Client credentials are secret tokens issued by the authorization server to clients in order to communicate with them.

Confidential client type

This is a client application that keeps passwords and other credentials securely or maintains them confidentially. In the Quora sign in using Twitter example, the Quora app server is secure and has restricted access implementation. Therefore, it is of the confidential client type. Only the Quora app administrator has access to client credentials.

Public client type

These are client applications that do *not* keep passwords and other credentials securely or maintain them confidentially. Any native app on mobile or desktop, or an app that runs on browser, are perfect examples of the public client type, as these keep client credentials embedded inside them. Hackers can crack these apps and the client credentials can be revealed.

A client can be a distributed component-based application, for example, it could have both a web browser component and a server-side component. In this case, both components will have different client types and security contexts. Such a client should register each component as a separate client if the authorization server does not support such clients.

Based on the OAuth 2.0 client types, a client can have the following profiles:

- Web application
- User agent-based application
- Native application

Web application

The Quora web application used in the Quora sign in using Twitter example is a perfect example of an OAuth 2.0 web application client profile. Quora is a confidential client running on a web server. The resource owner (end user) accesses the Quora application (OAuth 2.0 client) on the browser (user agent) using a HTML user interface on his device (desktop/tablet/cell phone). The resource owner cannot access the client (Quora OAuth 2.0 client) credentials and access tokens, as these are stored on the web server. You can see this behavior in the diagram of the OAuth 2.0 sample flow. See steps 6 to 8 in the following figure:

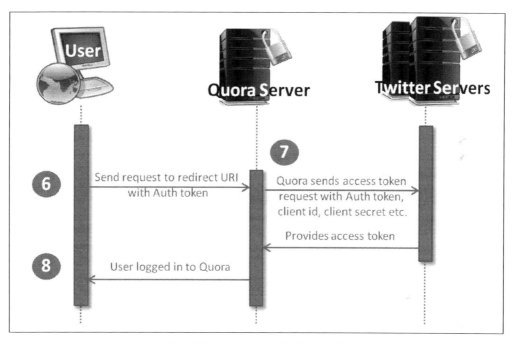

OAuth 2.0 client web application profile

User agent-based application

User agent-based applications are of the public client type. Here, though, the application resides in the web server, but the resource owner downloads it on the user agent (for example, a web browser) and then executes the application. Here, the downloaded application that resides in the user agent on the resource owner's device communicates with the authorization server. The resource owner can access the client credentials and access tokens. A gaming application is a good example of such an application profile.

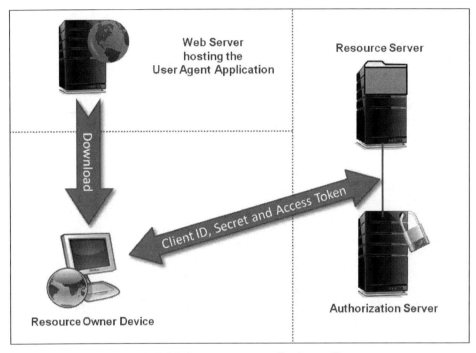

OAuth 2.0 client user agent application profile

Native application

Native applications are similar to user agent-based applications, except these are installed on the resource owner's device and execute natively, instead of being downloaded from the web server, and then executes inside the user agent. Many native clients (mobile apps) you download on your mobile are of the native application type. Here, the platform makes sure that other application on the device do not access the credentials and access tokens of other applications. In addition, native applications should not share client credentials and OAuth tokens with servers that communicate with native applications.

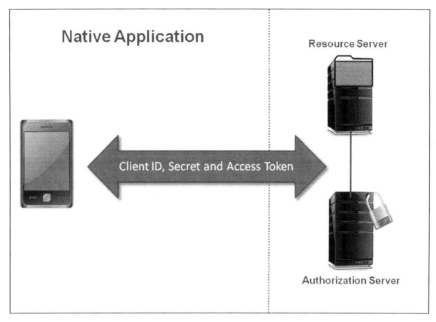

OAuth 2.0 client native application profile

Client identifier

It is the authorization server's responsibility to provide a unique identifier to the registered client. This client identifier is a string representation of the information provided by the registered client. The authorization server needs to make sure that this identifier is unique. The authorization server should not use it on its own for authentication.

The OAuth 2.0 specification does not specify the size of the client identifier. The authorization server can set the size, and it should document the size of the client identifier it issues.

Client authentication

The authorization server should authenticate the client based on their client type. The authorization server should determine the authentication method that suits and meets security requirements. It should only use one authentication method in each request.

Typically, the authorization server uses a set of client credentials, such as the client password and some key tokens, to authenticate confidential clients.

The authorization server may establish a client authentication method with public clients. However, it must not rely on this authentication method to identify the client, for security reasons.

A client possessing a client password can use basic HTTP authentication. OAuth 2.0 does not recommend sending client credentials in the request body. It recommends using TLS and brute force attack protection on endpoints required for authentication.

OAuth 2.0 protocol endpoints

An endpoint is nothing but a URI we use for REST or web components such as Servlet or JSP. OAuth 2.0 defines three types of endpoint. Two are authorization server endpoints and one is a client endpoint:

- Authorization endpoint (authorization server endpoint)
- Token endpoint (authorization server endpoint)
- Redirection endpoint (client endpoint)

Authorization endpoint

This endpoint is responsible for verifying the identity of the resource owner and, once verified, obtaining the authorization grant. We'll discuss the authorization grant in the next section.

The authorization server require TLS for the authorization endpoint. The endpoint URI must not include the fragment component. The authorization endpoint must support the HTTP GET method.

The specification does not specify the following:

- The way the authorization server authenticates the client.
- How the client will receive the authorization endpoint URI. Normally, documentation contains the authorization endpoint URI, or the client obtains it at the time of registration.

Token endpoint

The client calls the token endpoint to receive the access token by sending the authorization grant or refresh token. The token endpoint is used by all authorization grants except an implicit grant.

Like the authorization endpoint, the token endpoint also requires TLS. The client must use the HTTP POST method to make the request to the token endpoint.

Like the authorization endpoint, the specification does not specify how the client will receive the token endpoint URI.

Redirection endpoint

The authorization server redirects the resource owner's user agent (for example, a web browser) back to the client using the redirection endpoint, once the authorization endpoint's interactions are completed between the resource owner and the authorization server. The client provides the redirection endpoint at the time of registration. The redirection endpoint must be an absolute URI and not contain a fragment component.

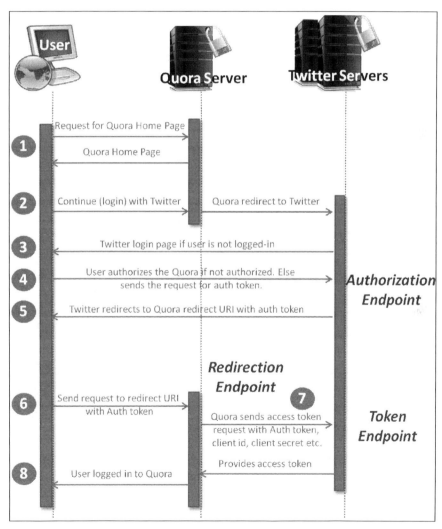

OAuth 2.0 endpoints

OAuth 2.0 grant types

The client requests an access token from the authorization server, based on the obtained authorization from the resource owner. The resource owner gives authorization in the form of an authorization grant. OAuth 2.0 defines four types of authorization grant:

- Authorization code grant
- Implicit grant
- Resource owner password credentials grant
- Client credentials grant

OAuth 2.0 also provides an extension mechanism to define additional grant types. You can explore this in the official OAuth 2.0 specifications.

Authorization code grant

The first sample flow that we discussed in the OAuth 2.0 example flow for signing in with Twitter depicts an authorization code grant. We'll add a few more steps for the complete flow. As you know, after the eighth step, the end user logs in to the Quora application. Let's assume the user is logging in to Quora for the first time and requests their Quora profile page:

1. After logging in, the Quora user clicks on their Quora profile page.
2. The OAuth client Quora requests the Quora user's (resource owner) resources (for example, Twitter profile photo and so on) from the Twitter resource server and sends the access token received in the previous step.
3. The Twitter resource server verifies the access token using the Twitter authorization server.
4. After successful validation of the access token, the Twitter resource server provides the requested resources to Quora (OAuth client).
5. Quora uses these resources and displays the Quora profile page of the end user.

Authorization code requests and responses

If you looked at all the steps (a total of 13) of the authorization code flow, you can see that there are a total of two requests made by the client to the authorization server, and the authorization server in reply provides two responses: one request-response for the authentication token and one request-response for the access token.

Let's discuss the parameters used for each of these requests and responses.

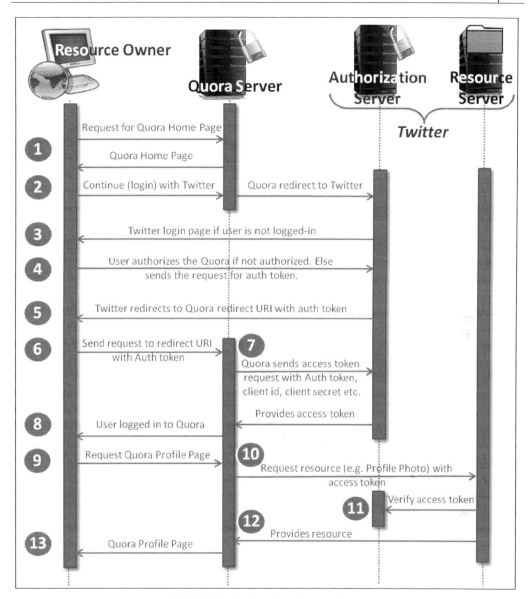

OAuth 2.0 authorization code grant flow

The authorization request (step 4) to the authorization endpoint URI:

Parameter	Required / Optional	Description
response_ type	Required	code (this value must be used).
client_id	Required	It represents the ID issued by the authorization server to the client at the time of registration.
redirect_ uri	Optional	It represents the redirect URI given by the client at the time of registration.
scope	Optional	The scope of the request. If not provided, then the authorization server provides the scope based on the defined policy.
state	Recommended	The client uses this parameter to maintain the client state between the requests and callback (from the authorization server). The specification recommends it to protect against cross site request forgery attacks.

Authorization response (step 5):

Parameter	Required / Optional	Description
code	Required	Code (authorization code) generated by the authorization server.
		Code should be expired after it is generated; the maximum recommended lifetime is 10 minutes.
		The client must not use the code more than once.
		If the client uses it more than once, then the request must be denied and all previous tokens issued based on the code should be revoked.
		Code is bound to the client ID and redirect URI.
state	Required	It represents the ID issued by the authorization server to the client at the time of registration.

Token request (step 7) to token endpoint URI:

Parameter	Required / Optional	Description
grant_type	Required	authorization_code (this value must be used).

Parameter	Required / Optional	Description
code	Required	Code (authorization code) received from the authorization server.
redirect_ uri	Required	Required if it was included in the authorization code request and the values should match.
client_id	Required	It represents the ID issued by the authorization server to the client at the time of registration.

Token response (step 8):

Parameter	Required / Optional	Description
access_ token	Required	The access token issued by the authorization server.
token_type	Required	The token type defined by the authorization server. Based on this, the client can utilize the access token. For example, bearer or mac.
refresh_ token	Optional	This token can be used by the client to get a new access token using the same authorization grant.
expires_in	Recommended	Denotes the lifetime of the access token in seconds. A value of 600 denotes 10 minutes of lifetime for the access token. If this parameter is not provided in the response, then the document should highlight the lifetime of the access token.
scope	Optional/ Required	Optional if identical to the scope requested by the client. Required if the access token scope is different from the one the client provided in their request to inform the client about the actual scope of the access token granted. If the client does not provide the scope while requesting the access token, then the authorization server should provide the default scope, or deny the request, indicating the invalid scope.

Error response:

Parameter	Required / Optional	Description
error	Required	One of the error codes defined in the specification, for example, unauthorized_client, invalid_ scope.
error_ description	Optional	Short description of the error.
error_uri	Optional	The URI of the error page describing the error.

An additional error parameter state is also sent in the error response if the state was passed in the client authorization request.

Implicit grant

The first sample flow that we discussed in the OAuth 2.0 example flow for signing in with Twitter depicts the authorization code grant. We'll add a few more steps for its complete flow. As you know after eighth steps, end user logs in to the Quora application. Let's assume user is logging in first time on Quora and requests for its Quora profile page:

1. *Step 9*: After login, the Quora user clicks on their Quora profile page.
2. *Step 10*: The OAuth client Quora requests the Quora user's (resource owner) resources (for example, Twitter profile photo and so on) from the Twitter resource server and sends the access token received in the previous step.
3. *Step 11*: The Twitter resource server verifies the access token using the Twitter authorization server.
4. *Step 12*: After successful validation of the access token, the Twitter resource server provides the requested resources to Quora (OAuth client).
5. *Step 13*: Quora uses these resources and displays the Quora profile page of the end user.

Implicit grant requests and responses

If you looked at all the steps (a total of 13) of the authorization code flow, you can see that there are total of two request made by the client to the authorization server, and the authorization server in reply provides two responses: one request-response for the authentication token and one request-response for the access token.

Let's discuss the parameters used for each of these requests and responses.

Authorization request to the authorization endpoint URI:

Parameter	Required / Optional	Description
`response_ type`	Required	Token (this value must be used).
`client_id`	Required	It represents the ID issued by the authorization server to the client at the time of registration.
`redirect_ uri`	Optional	It represents the redirect URI given by the client at the time of registration.
`scope`	Optional	The scope of the request. If not provided, then the authorization server provides the scope based on the defined policy.
`state`	Recommended	The client uses this parameter to maintain the client state between the requests and the callback (from the authorization server). The specification recommends it to protect against cross site request forgery attacks.

Access token response:

Parameter	Required / Optional	Description
`access_ token`	Required	The access token issued by the authorization server.
`token_type`	Required	The token type defined by the authorization server. Based on this, the client can utilize the access token. For example, bearer or mac.
`refresh_ token`	Optional	This token can be used by the client to get a new access token using the same authorization grant.
`expires_in`	Recommended	Denotes the lifetime of the access token in seconds. A value of 600 denotes 10 minutes of lifetime for the access token. If this parameter is not provided in the response, then the document should highlight the lifetime of the access token.

Parameter	Required / Optional	Description
scope	Optional/ Required	Optional if identical to the scope requested by the client. Required if the access token scope is different from the one the client provided in the request to inform the client about the actual scope of the access token granted. If the client does not provide the scope while requesting the access token, then the authorization server should provide the default scope, or deny the request, indicating the invalid scope.
State	Optional/ Requried	Required if the state was passed in the client authorization request.

Error response:

Parameter	Required / Optional	Description
error	Required	One of the error codes defined in the specification, for example, unauthorized_client, invalid_scope.
error_ description	Optional	Short description of the error.
error_uri	Optional	The URI of the error page describing the error.

An additional error parameter state is also sent in the error response if the state was passed in the client authorization request.

Resource owner password credentials grant

The first sample flow that we discussed in the OAuth 2.0 example flow for signing in with Twitter depicts the authorization code grant. We'll add a few more steps for its complete flow. As you know, after the eighth step, the end user logs in to the Quora application. Let's assume the user is logging in to Quora for the first time and requests their Quora profile page:

1. *Step 9*: After login, the Quora user clicks on their Quora profile page.
2. *Step 10*: The OAuth client Quora requests the Quora user's (resource owner) resources (for example, Twitter profile photo and so on) from the Twitter resource server and sends the access token received in the previous step.

3. *Step 11*: The Twitter resource server verifies the access token using the Twitter authorization server.

4. *Step 12*: After successful validation of the access token, the Twitter resource server provides the requested resources to Quora (OAuth client).

5. *Step 13*: Quora uses these resources and displays the Quora profile page of the end user.

Resource owner password credentials grant requests and responses.

As seen in the previous section, in all the steps (a total of 13) of the authorization code flow, you can see that there are total of two requests made by the client to the authorization server, and the authorization server in reply provides two responses: one request-response for the authentication token and one request-response for the access token.

Let's discuss the parameters used for each of these requests and responses.

Access token request to the token endpoint URI:

Parameter	Required / Optional	Description
grant_type	Required	Password (this value must be used).
username	Required	Username of the resource owner.
password	Required	Password of the resource owner.
scope	Optional	The scope of the request. If not provided, then the authorization server provides the scope based on the defined policy.

Access token response (step 8):

Parameter	Required / Optional	Description
access_ token	Required	The access token issued by the authorization server.
token_type	Required	The token type defined by the authorization server. Based on this, the client can utilize the access token. For example, bearer or mac.
refresh_ token	Optional	This token can be used by the client to get a new access token using the same authorization grant.

Parameter	Required / Optional	Description
expires_in	Recommended	Denotes the lifetime of the access token in seconds. A value of 600 denotes 10 minutes of lifetime for the access token. If this parameter is not provided in the response, then the document should highlight the lifetime of the access token.
Optional parameter	Optional	Additional parameter.

Client credentials grant

The first sample flow that we discussed in the OAuth 2.0 example flow for signing in with Twitter depicts the authorization code grant. We'll add a few more steps for its complete flow. As you know, after the eighth step, the end user logs in to the Quora application. Let's assume the user is logging in to Quora for the first time and requests their Quora profile page:

1. *Step 9*: After login, the Quora user clicks on their Quora profile page.
2. *Step 10*: The OAuth client Quora requests the Quora user's (resource owner) resources (for example, Twitter profile photo and so on) from the Twitter resource server and sends the access token received in the previous step.
3. *Step 11*: The Twitter resource server verifies the access token using the Twitter authorization server.
4. *Step 12*: After successful validation of the access token, the Twitter resource server provides the requested resources to Quora (OAuth client).
5. *Step 13*: Quora uses these resources and displays the Quora profile page of the end user.

Client credentials grant requests and responses.

If you looked at all the steps (a total of 13) of the authorization code flow, you can see that there are total of two requests made by the client to the authorization server, and the authorization server in reply provides two responses: one request-response for the authentication token and one request-response for the access token.

Let's discuss the parameters used for each of these requests and responses.

Access token request to the token endpoint URI:

Parameter	Required / Optional	Description
grant_type	Required	client_credentials (this value must be used).
scope	Optional	The scope of the request. If not provided, then the authorization server provides the scope based on the defined policy.

Access token response:

Parameter	Required / Optional	Description
access_token	Required	The access token issued by the authorization server.
token_type	Required	The token type defined by the authorization server. Based on this, the client can utilize the access token. For example, bearer or mac.
expires_in	Recommended	Denotes the lifetime of the access token in seconds. A value of 600 denotes 10 minutes of lifetime for the access token. If this parameter is not provided in the response, then the document should highlight the lifetime of the access token.

OAuth implementation using Spring Security

OAuth 2.0 is a way of securing APIs. Spring Security provides Spring Cloud Security and Spring Cloud OAuth2 components for implementing the rant flows we discussed above.

We'll create one more service, security-service, which will control authentication and authorization.

Create a new Maven project and follow these steps:

1. Add the Spring Security and Spring Security OAuth2 dependencies in pom.xml:

    ```
    <dependency>
     <groupId>org.springframework.cloud</groupId>
    ```

```
    <artifactId>spring-cloud-starter-security</artifactId>
</dependency>
<dependency>
    <groupId>org.springframework.cloud</groupId>
    <artifactId>spring-cloud-starter-oauth2</artifactId>
</dependency>
```

2. Use the @EnableResourceServer annotation in your application
    class. This will allow this application to work as a resource server.
    @EnableAuthorizationServer is another annotation we will use
    to enable the authorization server as per OAuth 2.0 specifications:

```
@SpringBootApplication
@RestController
@EnableResourceServer
public class SecurityApp {

    @RequestMapping("/user")
    public Principal user(Principal user) {
        return user;
    }

    public static void main(String[] args) {
        SpringApplication.run(SecurityApp.class, args);
    }

    @Configuration
    @EnableAuthorizationServer
    protected static class OAuth2Config extends
AuthorizationServerConfigurerAdapter {

        @Autowired
        private AuthenticationManager authenticationManager;

        @Override
        public void configure(AuthorizationServerEndpointsConfigur
er endpointsConfigurer) throws Exception {
                endpointsConfigurer.authenticationManager(authenticati
onManager);
        }

        @Override
        public void configure(ClientDetailsServiceConfigurer
clientDetailsServiceConfigurer) throws Exception {
    // Using hardcoded inmemory mechanism because it is just an
    example
```

```
        clientDetailsServiceConfigurer.inMemory()
         .withClient("acme")
         .secret("acmesecret")
         .authorizedGrantTypes("authorization_code", "refresh_
token", "implicit", "password", "client_credentials")
         .scopes("webshop");
      }
   }
}
```

3. Update the security-service configuration in `application.yml`, as shown in the following code:

   ○ `server.contextPath`: It denotes the context path.

   ○ `security.user.password`: We'll use the hardcoded password for this demonstration. You can re-configure it for real use:

```
application.yml
info:
    component:
        Security Server

server:
    port: 9001
    ssl:
        key-store: classpath:keystore.jks
        key-store-password: password
        key-password: password
    contextPath: /auth

security:
    user:
        password: password

logging:
    level:
        org.springframework.security: DEBUG
```

Now we have our security server in place, we'll expose our APIs using the new microservice `api-service`, which will be used for communicating with external applications and UIs.

Create a new Maven project and follow these steps:

1. Add the Spring Security and Spring Security OAuth2 dependencies in `pom.xml`:

```
<dependency>
   <groupId>org.springframework.boot</groupId>
   <artifactId>spring-boot-starter-undertow</artifactId>
</dependency>
<dependency>
   <groupId>org.springframework.boot</groupId>
   <artifactId>spring-boot-starter-actuator</artifactId>
</dependency>

<dependency>
   <groupId>com.packtpub.mmj</groupId>
   <artifactId>online-table-reservation-common</artifactId>
   <version>PACKT-SNAPSHOT</version>
</dependency>
<dependency>
   <groupId>org.springframework.cloud</groupId>
   <artifactId>spring-cloud-starter-security</artifactId>
</dependency>
<dependency>
   <groupId>org.springframework.cloud</groupId>
   <artifactId>spring-cloud-starter-oauth2</artifactId>
</dependency>
<dependency>
   <groupId>org.springframework.cloud</groupId>
   <artifactId>spring-cloud-starter-eureka</artifactId>
</dependency>
<dependency>
   <groupId>org.springframework.cloud</groupId>
   <artifactId>spring-cloud-starter-hystrix</artifactId>
</dependency>
<dependency>
   <groupId>org.springframework.cloud</groupId>
   <artifactId>spring-cloud-starter-bus-amqp</artifactId>
</dependency>
<dependency>
   <groupId>org.springframework.cloud</groupId>
   <artifactId>spring-cloud-starter-stream-rabbit</artifactId>
</dependency>
<dependency>
   <groupId>org.apache.httpcomponents</groupId>
```

```
      <artifactId>httpclient</artifactId>
  </dependency>
  <dependency>
      <groupId>org.springframework.boot</groupId>
      <artifactId>spring-boot-starter-web</artifactId>
  </dependency>
  <dependency>
      <!-- Testing starter -->
      <groupId>org.springframework.boot</groupId>
      <artifactId>spring-boot-starter-test</artifactId>
  </dependency>
```

2. Use the `@EnableResourceServer` annotation in your application class.
   This will allow this application to work as a resource server:

```
@SpringBootApplication
@EnableDiscoveryClient
@EnableCircuitBreaker
@EnableResourceServer
@ComponentScan({"com.packtpub.mmj.api.service", "com.packtpub.mmj.
common"})
public class ApiApp {

    private static final Logger LOG = LoggerFactory.
getLogger(ApiApp.class);

    static {
        // for localhost testing only
        LOG.warn("Will now disable hostname check in SSL, only to
be used during development");
        HttpsURLConnection.setDefaultHostnameVerifier((hostname,
sslSession) -> true);
    }

    @Value("${app.rabbitmq.host:localhost}")
    String rabbitMqHost;

    @Bean
    public ConnectionFactory connectionFactory() {
        LOG.info("Create RabbitMqCF for host: {}", rabbitMqHost);
        CachingConnectionFactory connectionFactory = new CachingCo
nnectionFactory(rabbitMqHost);
        return connectionFactory;
    }

    public static void main(String[] args) {
```

```
        LOG.info("Register MDCHystrixConcurrencyStrategy");
        HystrixPlugins.getInstance().
registerConcurrencyStrategy(new MDCHystrixConcurrencyStrategy());
        SpringApplication.run(ApiApp.class, args);
    }
}
```

3. Update the `api-service` configuration in `application.yml`, as shown in the following code:

    ○   `security.oauth2.resource.userInfoUri`: It denotes the security service user URI.

    ```
    application.yml
    info:
      component: API Service

    spring:
      application:
          name: api-service
      aop:
          proxyTargetClass: true

    server:
      port: 7771

    security:
      oauth2:
        resource:
         userInfoUri: https://localhost:9001/auth/user

    management:
      security:
        enabled: false
    ## Other properties like Eureka, Logging and so on
    ```

Now we have our security server in place, we'll expose our APIs using the new microservice `api-service`, which will be used for communicating with external applications and UIs.

Now let's test and explore how it works for different OAuth 2.0 grant types.

 We'll make use of the `postman` extension to the Chrome browser to test the different flows.

Authorization code grant

We will enter the following URL in our browser. A request for authorization code is as follows:

```
https://localhost:9001/auth/oauth/authorize?response_
type=code&client_id=client&redirect_uri=http://localhost:7771/1&scope
=apiAccess&state=1234
```

Here, we provide the client ID (hardcoded client is by default we have registered in our security service), redirect URI, scope (hardcoded value `apiAccess` in security service) and state. You must be wondering about the `state` parameter. It contains the random number that we re-validate in response to prevent cross site request forgery.

If the resource owner (user) is not already authenticated, it will ask for the user name and password. Provide user as the `username` and password as the `password`; we have hardcoded these values in security service.

Once the login is successful, it will ask to provide your (resource owner) approval:

OAuth 2.0 authorization code grant – resource grant approval

Select **Approve** and click on **Authorize**. This action will redirect the application to `http://localhost:7771/1?code=o8t4fi&state=1234`.

As you can see, it has returned the authorization code and state.

Now, we'll use this code to retrieve the access code. We'll use the postman Chrome extension. First we'll add the authorization header using **Username** as `client` and **Password** as `clientsecret`, as shown in the following screenshot:

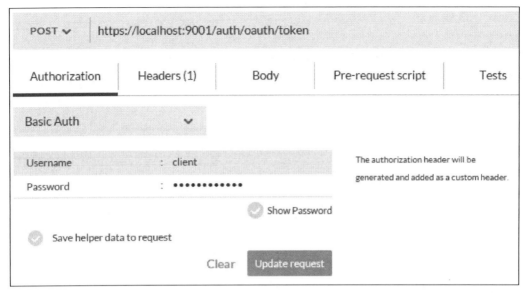

OAuth 2.0 authorization code grant – access token request – adding the authentication

This will add the **Authorization** header to the request with the value `Basic Y2xpZW50OmNsaWVudHNlY3JldA==`.

Now, we'll add a few other parameters to the request, as shown in the following screenshot, and then submit the request:

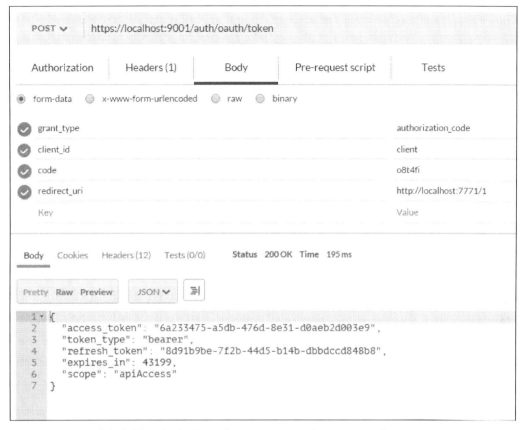

OAuth 2.0 authorization code grant – access token request and response

This returns the following response, as per the OAuth 2.0 specification:

```
{
  "access_token": "6a233475-a5db-476d-8e31-d0aeb2d003e9",
  "token_type": "bearer",
  "refresh_token": "8d91b9be-7f2b-44d5-b14b-dbbdccd848b8",
  "expires_in": 43199,
  "scope": "apiAccess"
}
```

Now we can use this information to access the resources owned by the resource owner. For example, if `https://localhost:8765/api/restaurant/1` represents the restaurant with the ID of 1, then it should return the respective restaurant details.

Without the access token, if we enter the URL, it returns the error `Unauthorized`, with the message `Full authentication is required to access this resource`.

Now, let's access this URL with the access token, as shown in the following screenshot:

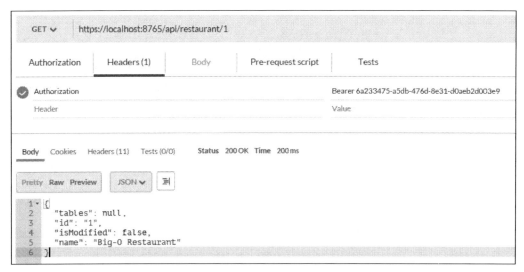

OAuth 2.0 authorization code grant – using the access token for API access

As you can see, we have added the **Authorization** header with the access token.

Now, we will explore implicit grant implementation.

Implicit grant

Implicit grants are very similar to authorization code grants, except for the code grant step. If you remove the first step—the code grant step (where the client application receives the authorization token from the authorization server)—from the authorization code grant, the rest of the steps are the same. Let's check it out.

Enter the following URL and parameters in the browser and press *Enter*. Also, make sure to add basic authentication, with client as the `username` and password as the `password` if asked:

```
https://localhost:9001/auth/oauth/authorize?response_
type=token&redirect_uri=https://localhost:8765&scope=apiAccess&state=
553344&client_id=client
```

Here, we are calling the authorization endpoint with the following request parameters: Response type, client ID, redirect URI, scope, and state.

When the request is successful, the browser will be redirected to the following URL with new request parameters and values:

```
https://localhost:8765/#access_token=6a233475-a5db-476d-8e31-
d0aeb2d003e9&token_type=bearer&state=553344&expires_in=19592
```

Here, we receive the `access_token`, `token_type`, state, and expiry duration for the token. Now, we can make use of this access token to access the APIs, as used in the authorization code grant.

Resource owner password credential grant

In this grant, we provide the `username` and `password` as parameters when requesting the access token, along with the `grant_type`, `client`, and `scope` parameters. We also need to use the client ID and secret to authenticate the request. These grant flows use client applications in place of browsers, and are normally used in mobile and desktop apps.

In the following postman tool screenshot, the authorization header has already been added using basic authentication with `client_id` and `password`:

OAuth 2.0 resource owner password credentials grant – access token request and response

Once the access token is received by the client, it can be used in a similar way to how it is used in the authorization code grant.

Client credentials grant

In this flow, the client provides their own credentials and retrieves the access token. It does not use the resource owner's credentials and permissions.

As you can see in the following screenshot, we directly enter the token endpoint with only two parameters: grant_type and scope. The authorization header is added using client_id and client secret:

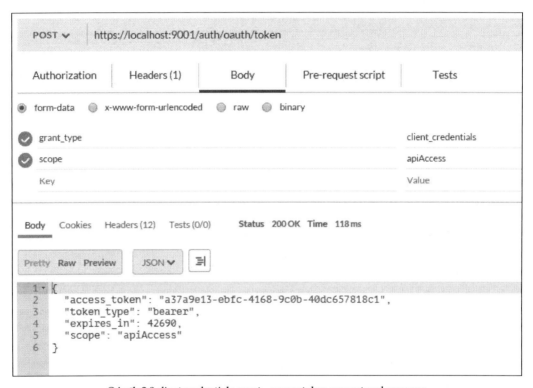

OAuth 2.0 client credentials grant – access token request and response

You can use the access token similarly as it is explained for the authorization code grant.

References

For more information, you refer to these links:

- *RESTful Java Web Services Security, Packt Publishing,* by René Enríquez, Andrés Salazar C: `https://www.packtpub.com/application-development/restful-java-web-services-security`

- *Spring Security [Video], Packt Publishing*: `https://www.packtpub.com/application-development/spring-security-video`

- The OAuth 2.0 Authorization Framework: `https://tools.ietf.org/html/rfc6749`

- Spring Security: `http://projects.spring.io/spring-security`

- Spring OAuth2: `http://projects.spring.io/spring-security-oauth/`

Summary

In this chapter, we have learned how important it is to have the TLS layer or HTTPS in place for all web traffic. We have added a self-signed certificate to our sample application. I would like to reiterate that, for a production application, you must use the certificates offered by certificate signing authorities. We have also explored the fundamentals of OAuth 2.0 and various OAuth 2.0 grant flows. Different OAuth 2.0 grant flows are implemented using Spring Security and OAuth 2.0. In the next chapter, we'll implement the UI for the sample OTRS project and will explore how all the components work together.

7
Consuming Services Using a Microservice Web App

Now, after developing the microservices, it would be interesting to see how the services offered by the **Online Table Reservation System (OTRS)** could be consumed by web or mobile applications. We will develop the web application (UI) using AngularJS/bootstrap to build the prototype of the web application. This sample application will display the data and flow of this sample project – a small utility project. This web application will also be a sample project and will run independently. Earlier, web applications were being developed in single web archives (files with .war extensions) that contain both UI and server-side code. The reason for doing so was pretty simple as UI was also developed using Java with JSPs, servlets, JSF, and so on. Nowadays, UIs are being developed independently using JavaScript. Therefore, these UI apps also deploy as a single microservice. In this chapter, we'll explore how these independent UI applications are being developed. We will develop and implement the OTRS sample app without login and authorization flow. We'll deploy a very limited functionality implementation and cover the high level AngularJS concepts. For more information on AngularJS, you can refer to *AngularJS by Example, Chandermani, Packt publishing.*

In this chapter, we will cover the following topics:

- AngularJS framework overview
- Development of OTRS features
- Setting up a web app (UI)

AngularJS framework overview

Now since we are ready with our HTML5 web app setup, we can go through the basics of AngularJS. This will help us to understand the AngularJS code. This section depicts the high level of understanding that you can utilize to understand the sample app and explore further using AngularJS documentation or by referring to other Packt publications.

AngularJS is a client side JavaScript framework. It is flexible enough to be used as a **MVC (Model View Controller)** or **MVVM (Model-View-ViewModel)**. It also provides built-in services like $http or $log using a dependency injection pattern.

MVC

MVC is well-known design pattern. Struts and Spring MVC are popular examples. Let's see how they fit in the JavaScript world:

- **Model**: Models are JavaScript objects that contain the application data. They also represent the state of the application.

- **View**: View is a presentation layer that consists of HTML files. Here, you can show the data from models and provide the interactive interface to the user.

- **Controller**: You can define the controller in JavaScript and it contains the application logic.

MVVM

MVVM is an architecture design pattern that specifically targets the UI development. MVVM is designed to make two-way data binding easier. Two-way data binding provides the synchronization between the Model and View. When the Model (data) changes, it reflects immediately on the View. Similarly, when the user changes the data on the View, it reflects on the Model.

- **Model**: This is very similar to MVC and contains the business logic and data.

- **View**: Like MVC, it contains the presentation logic or user interface.

- **ViewModel**: ViewModel contains the data binding between the View and Model. Therefore, it is an interface between the View and Model.

Modules

A module is the first thing we define for any AngularJS application. A module is a container that contains the different parts of the app such as controllers, services, filters, and so on. An AngularJS app can be written in a single module or multiple modules. An AngularJS module can contain other modules also.

Many other JavaScript frameworks use the `main` method for instantiating and wiring the different parts of the app. AngularJS does not have the `main` method. It uses the module as an entry point due to following reasons:

- **Modularity**: You can divide and create your application feature-wise or with reusable components.

- **Simplicity**: You might have come across complex and large application code, which makes maintenance and enhancement a headache. No more, AngularJS makes code simple, readable, and easy to understand.

- **Testing**: It makes unit testing and end-to-end testing easier as you can override configuration and load only those modules which are required.

Each AngularJS app needs to have a single module for bootstrapping the AngularJS app. Bootstrapping our app requires the following three parts:

- **App module**: A JavaScript file (`app.js`) that contains the AngularJS module as shown:

  ```
  var otrsApp = AngularJS.module('otrsApp', [ ])
  // [] contains the reference to other modules
  ```

- **Loading Angular library and app module**: An `index.html` file containing the reference to the JavaScript file with other AngularJS libraries:

  ```
  <script type="text/javascript" src="AngularJS/AngularJS.js"/>
  <script type="text/javascript" src="scripts/app.js"/></script>
  ```

- **App DOM configuration**: This tells the AngularJS location of the DOM element where bootstrapping should take place. It can be done in either of two ways:

  - `Index.html` file that also contains an HTML element (typically `<html>`) with the `ng-app` (AngularJS directive) attribute having the value given in `app.js`. AngularJS directives are prefixed with ng (AngularJS): `<html lang="en" ng-app="otrsApp" class="no-js">`.

  - Or use this command if you are loading the JavaScript files asynchronously: `AngularJS.bootstrap(document.documentElement, ['otrsApp']);`.

An AngularJS module has two important parts, `config()` and `run()`, apart from other components like controllers, services, filters, and so on.

- `config()` is used for registering and configuring the modules and it only entertains the providers and constants using `$injector`. `$injector` is an AngularJS service. We'll cover providers and `$injector` in the next section. You cannot use instances here. It prevents the use of services before it is fully configured.

- `run()` is used for executing the code after `$injector` is created using the preceding config method. This only entertains the instances and constants. You cannot use providers here to avoid configuration at run time.

Providers and services

Let's have a look at the following code:

```
.controller('otrsAppCtrl', function ($injector) {
var log = $injector.get('$log');
```

`$log` is an inbuilt AngularJS service that provides the logging API. Here, we are using another inbuilt service, `$injector`, that allows us to use the `$log` service. `$injector` is an argument in the controller. AngularJS uses function definitions and regex to provide the `$injector` service to a caller, also known as the controller. These are examples of how AngularJS effectively uses the dependency injection pattern.

AngularJS heavily uses the dependency injection pattern. AngularJS uses the injector service (`$injector`) to instantiate and wire most of the objects we use in our AngularJS app. This injector creates two types of objects – services and specialized objects.

For simplification, you can say that we (developers) define services. On the contrary, specialized objects are AngularJS stuff like controllers, filters, directives, and so on.

AngularJS provides five recipe types that tell the injector how to create service objects – **provider, value, factory, service,** and **constant**.

- The provider is the core and most complex recipe type. Other recipes are synthetic sugar on it. We generally avoid using the provider except when we need to create reusable code that requires global configuration.

- The value and constant recipe types works as their name suggests. Both cannot have dependencies. Moreover, the difference between them lies with their usage. You cannot use value service objects in the configuration phase.

- The factory and service are the most used services types. They are of a similar type. We use the factory recipe when we want to produce JavaScript primitives and functions. On the other hand, the service is used when we want to produce custom defined types.

As we have now some understanding of services, we can say that there are two common uses of services – organizing code and sharing code across apps. Services are singleton objects, which are lazily instantiated by the AngularJS service factory. By now, we have already seen a few of the in-built AngularJS services like $injector, $log, and so on. AngularJS services are prefixed with the $ symbol.

Scopes

In AngularJS apps, two types of scopes are widely used: $rootScope and $scope:

- $rootScope is the top most object in the scope hierarchy and has the global scope associated with it. That means that any variable you attached to it will be available everywhere and therefore use of $rootScope should be a carefully considered decision.

- Controllers have $scope as an argument in the callback function. It is used for binding data from the controller to the view. Its scope is limited to the use of the controller it is associated with.

Controllers

The controller is defined by the JavaScript constructor function as having a $scope as an argument. The controller's main purpose is to tie the data to the view. The controller function is also used for writing business logic – setting up the initial state of the $scope object and adding the behavior to $scope. The controller signature looks like the following:

```
RestModule.controller('RestaurantsCtrl', function ($scope,
restaurantService) {
```

Here, the controller is a part of RestModule. The name of the controller is RestaurantCtrl. $scope and restaurantService are passed as arguments.

Filters

The purpose of filters is to format the value of a given expression. In the following code we have defined the `datetime1` filter that takes date as an argument and changes the value in *dd MMM yyyy HH:mm* format like *04 Apr 2016 04:13 PM*.

```
.filter('datetime1', function ($filter) {
    return function (argDateTime) {
        if (argDateTime) {
            return $filter('date')(new Date(argDateTime), 'dd MMM yyyy
HH:mm a');
        }
        return "";
    };
});
```

Directives

As we have seen in the *Modules* section, AngularJS directives are HTML attributes with an `ng` prefix. Some of the popular directives are:

- `ng-app`: This directive defines the AngularJS application
- `ng-model`: This directive binds the HTML form input to data
- `ng-bind`: This directive binds the data to the HTML view
- `ng-submit`: This directive submits the HTML form
- `ng-repeat`: This directive iterates the collection
  ```
  <div ng-app="">
      <p>Search: <input type="text" ng-model="searchValue"></p>
      <p ng-bind="searchedTerm"></p>
  </div>
  ```

UI-Router

In **single page applications (SPAs)**, the page only loads once and the user navigates through different links without page refresh. It is all possible because of routing. Routing is a way to make SPA navigation feel like a normal site. Therefore, routing is very important for SPA.

The AngularUI team built UI-Router, an AngularJS routing framework. UI-Router is not a part of core AngularJS. UI-Router not only changes the route URL, but it also changes the state of the application when the user clicks on any link in the SPA. Because UI-Router can also make state changes, you can change the view of the page without changing the URL. This is possible because of the application state management by UI-Router.

If we consider the SPA as a state machine then the state is a current state of the application. We will use the attribute `ui-sref` in a HTML link tag when we create the route link. The attribute `href` in the link will be generated from this and point to certain states of the application which are created in `app.js`.

We use the `ui-view` attribute in the HTML div to use UI-Router: for example, `<div ui-view></div>`.

Development of OTRS features

As you know, we are developing the SPA. Therefore, once the application loads, you can perform all the operations without page refresh. All interactions with the server are performed using AJAX calls. Now, we'll make use of the AngularJS concepts that we have covered in the first section. We'll cover the following scenarios:

- A page that will display a list of restaurants. This will also be our home page.
- Search restaurants.
- Restaurant details with reservation options.
- Login (not from the server, but used for displaying the flow).
- Reservation confirmation.

For the home page, we will create `index.html` and a template that will contain the restaurant listing in the middle section or the content area.

Home page/restaurant list page

The home page is the main page of any web application. To design the home page, we are going to use the Angular-UI bootstrap rather than the actual bootstrap. Angular-UI is an Angular version of the bootstrap. The home page will be divided into three sections:

- The header section will contain the app name, search restaurants form, and user name at top-right corner.

- The content or middle section will contain the restaurant listing which will have the restaurant name as the link. This link will point to the restaurant details and reservation page.
- The footer section will contain the app name with the copyright mark.

You must be interested in viewing the home page before designing or implementing it. Therefore, let us first see how it will look like once we have our content ready:

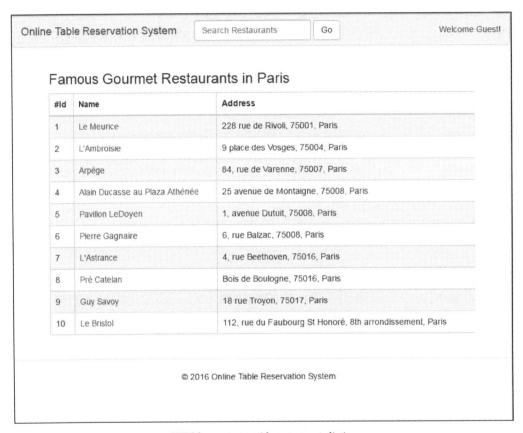

OTRS home page with restaurants listing

Now, to design our home page, we need to add following four files:

- `index.html`: Our main HTML file
- `app.js`: Our main AngularJS module
- `restaurants.js`: The restaurants module that also contains the restaurant Angular service
- `restaurants.html`: The HTML template that will display the list of restaurants

index.html

First, we'll add the `./app/index.html` in our project workspace. The contents of `index.html` will be as explained here onwards.

 I have added comments in between the code to make the code more readable and make it easier to understand.

`index.html` is divided into many parts. We'll discuss a few of the key parts here. First, we will see how to address old Internet Explorer versions. If you want to target the Internet Explorer browser versions greater than 8 or IE version 9 onwards, then we need to add following block that will prevent JavaScript rendering and give the no-js output to the end-user.

```
<!--[if lt IE 7]>        <html lang="en" ng-app="otrsApp" class="no-js
lt-ie9 lt-ie8 lt-ie7"> <![endif]-->
<!--[if IE 7]>           <html lang="en" ng-app="otrsApp" class="no-js
lt-ie9 lt-ie8"> <![endif]-->
<!--[if IE 8]>           <html lang="en" ng-app="otrsApp" class="no-js
lt-ie9"> <![endif]-->
<!--[if gt IE 8]><!--> <html lang="en" ng-app="otrsApp" class="no-js">
<!--<![endif]-->
```

Then, after adding a few meta tags and the title of the application, we'll also define the important meta `tag` viewport. The viewport is used for responsive UI designs.

The `width` property defined in the content attribute controls the size of the viewport. It can be set to a specific number of pixels like `width = 600` or to the special value device-width value which is the width of the screen in CSS pixels at a scale of 100%.

The initial-scale property controls the zoom level when the page is first loaded. The maximum-scale, minimum-scale, and user-scalable properties control how users are allowed to zoom the page in or out.

```
<meta name="viewport" content="width=device-width, initial-
scale=1">
```

In the next few lines, we'll define the style sheets of our application. We are adding `normalize.css` and `main.css` from HTML5 boilerplate code. We are also adding our application's customer CSS `app.css`. Finally, we are adding the bootstrap 3 CSS. Apart from the customer `app.css`, other CSS are referenced in it. There is no change in these CSS files.

```
<link rel="stylesheet" href="bower_components/html5-boilerplate/dist/
css/normalize.css">
```

```
        <link rel="stylesheet" href="bower_components/html5-
boilerplate/dist/css/main.css">
        <link rel="stylesheet" href="public/css/app.css">
        <link data-require="bootstrap-css@*" data-server="3.0.0"
rel="stylesheet" href="//netdna.bootstrapcdn.com/bootstrap/3.0.0/css/
bootstrap.min.css" />
```

Then we'll define the scripts using the `script` tag. We are adding the modernizer, Angular, Angular-route, and our own developed custom JavaScript file `app.js`. We have already discussed Angular and Angular-UI. `app.js` will be discussed in the next section.

Modernizer allows web developers to use new CSS3 and HTML5 features while maintaining a fine level of control over browsers that don't support them. Basically, modernizer performs the next generation feature detection (checking the availability of those features) while the page loads in the browser and reports the results. Based on these results you can detect what are the latest features available in the browser and based on that you can provide an interface to the end user. If the browser does not support a few of the features then an alternate flow or UI is provided to the end user.

We are also adding the bootstrap templates which are written in JavaScript using the `ui-bootstrap-tpls javascript` file.

```
        <script src="bower_components/html5-boilerplate/dist/js/
vendor/modernizr-2.8.3.min.js"></script>
        <script src="bower_components/angular/angular.min.js"></
script>
        <script src="bower_components/angular-route/angular-route.min.
js"></script>
        <script src="app.js"></script>
      <script data-require="ui-bootstrap@0.5.0" data-semver="0.5.0"
src="http://angular-ui.github.io/bootstrap/ui-bootstrap-tpls-
0.6.0.js"></script>
```

We can also add style to the `head` tag as shown in the following. This style allows drop-down menus to work.

```
        <style>
          div.navbar-collapse.collapse {
              display: block;
              overflow: hidden;
              max-height: 0px;
              -webkit-transition: max-height .3s ease;
              -moz-transition: max-height .3s ease;
              -o-transition: max-height .3s ease;
              transition: max-height .3s ease;
```

```
        }
        div.navbar-collapse.collapse.in {
            max-height: 2000px;
        }
    </style>
```

In the `body` tag we are defining the controller of the application using the `ng-controller` attribute. While the page loads, it tells the controller the name of the application to Angular.

```
        <body ng-controller="otrsAppCtrl">
```

Then, we define the `header` section of the home page. In the `header` section, we'll define the application title, `Online Table Reservation System`. Also, we'll define the search form that will search the restaurants.

```
    <!-- BEGIN HEADER -->
        <nav class="navbar navbar-default" role="navigation">

            <div class="navbar-header">
                <a class="navbar-brand" href="#">
                    Online Table Reservation System
                </a>
            </div>
            <div class="collapse navbar-collapse" ng-
class="!navCollapsed && 'in'" ng-click="navCollapsed = true">
                <form class="navbar-form navbar-left" role="search"
ng-submit="search()">
                    <div class="form-group">
                        <input type="text" id="searchedValue" ng-
model="searchedValue" class="form-control" placeholder="Search
Restaurants">
                    </div>
                    <button type="submit" class="btn btn-default" ng-
click="">Go</button>
                </form>
        <!-- END HEADER -->
```

Then, in the next section, the middle section, includes where we actually bind the different views, marked with actual content comments. The `ui-view` attribute in `div` gets its content dynamically from Angular such as restaurant details, restaurant list, and so on. We have also added a warning dialog and spinner to the middle section that will be visible as and when required.

```
        <div class="clearfix"></div>
        <!-- BEGIN CONTAINER -->
```

```
        <div class="page-container container">
            <!-- BEGIN CONTENT -->
            <div class="page-content-wrapper">
                <div class="page-content">
                    <!-- BEGIN ACTUAL CONTENT -->
                    <div ui-view class="fade-in-up"></div>
                    <!-- END ACTUAL CONTENT -->
                </div>
            </div>
            <!-- END CONTENT -->
        </div>
        <!-- loading spinner -->
        <div id="loadingSpinnerId" ng-show="isSpinnerShown()"
 style="top:0; left:45%; position:absolute; z-index:999">
            <script type="text/ng-template" id="alert.html">
                <div class="alert alert-warning" role="alert">
                <div ng-transclude></div>
                </div>
            </script>
            <uib-alert type="warning" template-url="alert.
 html"><b>Loading...</b></uib-alert>
        </div>
        <!-- END CONTAINER -->
```

The final section of the `index.html` is the footer. Here, we are just adding the static content and copyright text. You can add whatever content you want here.

```
        <!-- BEGIN FOOTER -->
        <div class="page-footer">
            <hr/><div style="padding: 0 39%">&copy; 2016 Online Table
 Reservation System</div>
        </div>
        <!-- END FOOTER -->
    </body>
</html>
```

app.js

`app.js` is our main application file. Because we have defined it in `index.html`, it gets loaded as soon as our `index.html` is called.

 We need to take care that we do not mix, route (URI) with REST endpoints. Routes represents the state/view of the SPA.

As we are using the Edge Server (Proxy Server), everything will be accessible from it including our REST endpoints. External applications including the UI will use the Edge Server host to access the application. You can configure it in some global constants file and then use it wherever it is required. This will allow you to configure the REST host at a single place and use it at other places.

```
'use strict';
/*
This call initializes our application and registers all the modules,
which are passed as an array in the second argument.
*/
var otrsApp = angular.module('otrsApp', [
    'ui.router',
    'templates',
    'ui.bootstrap',
    'ngStorage',
    'otrsApp.httperror',
    'otrsApp.login',
    'otrsApp.restaurants'
])
/*
  Then we have defined the default route /restaurants
*/
        .config([
            '$stateProvider', '$urlRouterProvider',
            function ($stateProvider, $urlRouterProvider) {
                $urlRouterProvider.otherwise('/restaurants');
            }])
/*
    This functions controls the flow of the application and handles
the events.
*/
        .controller('otrsAppCtrl', function ($scope, $injector,
restaurantService) {
            var controller = this;

            var AjaxHandler = $injector.get('AjaxHandler');
            var $rootScope = $injector.get('$rootScope');
            var log = $injector.get('$log');
            var sessionStorage = $injector.get('$sessionStorage');
            $scope.showSpinner = false;
/*
    This function gets called when the user searches any restaurant.
It uses the Angular restaurant service that we'll define in the next
section to search the given search string.
```

```
*/
            $scope.search = function () {
                $scope.restaurantService = restaurantService;
                restaurantService.async().then(function () {
                    $scope.restaurants = restaurantService.
search($scope.searchedValue);
                });
            }
/*
    When the state is changed, the new controller controls the flows
based on the view and configuration and the existing controller is
destroyed. This function gets a call on the destroy event.
*/
            $scope.$on('$destroy', function destroyed() {
                log.debug('otrsAppCtrl destroyed');
                controller = null;
                $scope = null;
            });

            $rootScope.fromState;
            $rootScope.fromStateParams;
            $rootScope.$on('$stateChangeSuccess', function (event,
toState, toParams, fromState, fromStateParams) {
                $rootScope.fromState = fromState;
                $rootScope.fromStateParams = fromStateParams;
            });

            // utility method
            $scope.isLoggedIn = function () {
                if (sessionStorage.session) {
                    return true;
                } else {
                    return false;
                }
            };

            /* spinner status */
            $scope.isSpinnerShown = function () {
                return AjaxHandler.getSpinnerStatus();
            };

        })
/*
    This function gets executed when this object loads. Here we are
setting the user object which is defined for the root scope.
```

```
*/
            .run(['$rootScope', '$injector', '$state', function
    ($rootScope, $injector, $state) {
                    $rootScope.restaurants = null;
                    // self reference
                    var controller = this;
                    // inject external references
                    var log = $injector.get('$log');
                    var $sessionStorage = $injector.
    get('$sessionStorage');
                    var AjaxHandler = $injector.get('AjaxHandler');

                    if (sessionStorage.currentUser) {
                        $rootScope.currentUser = $sessionStorage.
    currentUser;
                    } else {
                        $rootScope.currentUser = "Guest";
                        $sessionStorage.currentUser = ""
                    }
                }])
```

restaurants.js

`restaurants.js` represents an Angular service for our app which we'll use for the restaurants. We know that there are two common uses of services – organizing code and sharing code across apps. Therefore, we have created a restaurants service which will be used among different modules like search, list, details, and so on.

 Services are singleton objects, which are lazily instantiated by the AngularJS service factory.

The following section initializes the restaurant service module and loads the required dependencies.

```
angular.module('otrsApp.restaurants', [
    'ui.router',
    'ui.bootstrap',
    'ngStorage',
    'ngResource'
])
```

In the configuration, we are defining the routes and state of the `otrsApp.restaurants` module using UI-Router.

First we define the `restaurants` state by passing the JSON object containing the URL that points the router URI, the template URL that points to the HTML template that display the `restaurants` state, and the controller that will handle the events on the `restaurants` view.

On top of the `restaurants` view (route - /restaurants), a nested state `restaurants.profile` is also defined that will represent the specific restaurant. For example, /restaurant/1 would open and display the restaurant profile (details) page of a restaurant which is represented by `Id` 1. This state is called when a link is clicked in the `restaurants` template. In this `ui-sref="restaurants.profile({id: rest.id})"` rest represents the `restaurant` object retrieved from the `restaurants` view.

Notice that the state name is `'restaurants.profile'` which tells the AngularJS UI Router that the profile is a nested state of the `restaurants` state.

```
.config([
    '$stateProvider', '$urlRouterProvider',
    function ($stateProvider, $urlRouterProvider) {
        $stateProvider.state('restaurants', {
            url: '/restaurants',
            templateUrl: 'restaurants/restaurants.html',
            controller: 'RestaurantsCtrl'
        })
                // Restaurant show page
                .state('restaurants.profile', {
                    url: '/:id',
                    views: {
                        '@': {
                            templateUrl: 'restaurants/
restaurant.html',
                            controller: 'RestaurantCtrl'
                        }
                    }
                });
    }])
```

In the next code section, we are defining the restaurant service using the Angular factory service type. This restaurant service on load fetches the list of restaurants from the server using a REST call. It provides a list and searches restaurant operations and restaurant data.

```
.factory('restaurantService', function ($injector, $q) {
    var log = $injector.get('$log');
    var ajaxHandler = $injector.get('AjaxHandler');
    var deffered = $q.defer();
```

```
            var restaurantService = {};
            restaurantService.restaurants = [];
            restaurantService.orignalRestaurants = [];
            restaurantService.async = function () {
                ajaxHandler.startSpinner();
                if (restaurantService.restaurants.length === 0) {
                    ajaxHandler.get('/api/restaurant')
                            .success(function (data, status, headers,
config) {
                                log.debug('Getting restaurants');
                                sessionStorage.apiActive = true;
                                log.debug("if Restaurants --> " +
restaurantService.restaurants.length);
                                restaurantService.restaurants = data;
                                ajaxHandler.stopSpinner();
                                deffered.resolve();
                            })
                            .error(function (error, status, headers,
config) {
                                restaurantService.restaurants =
mockdata;
                                ajaxHandler.stopSpinner();
                                deffered.resolve();
                            });
                    return deffered.promise;
                } else {
                    deffered.resolve();
                    ajaxHandler.stopSpinner();
                    return deffered.promise;
                }
            };
            restaurantService.list = function () {
                return restaurantService.restaurants;
            };
            restaurantService.add = function () {
                console.log("called add");
                restaurantService.restaurants.push(
                        {
                            id: 103,
                            name: 'Chi Cha\'s Noodles',
                            address: '13 W. St., Eastern Park, New
County, Paris',
                        });
            };
```

```
restaurantService.search = function (searchedValue) {
    ajaxHandler.startSpinner();
    if (!searchedValue) {
        if (restaurantService.orignalRestaurants.length >
0) {
            restaurantService.restaurants =
restaurantService.orignalRestaurants;
        }
        deffered.resolve();
        ajaxHandler.stopSpinner();
        return deffered.promise;
    } else {
        ajaxHandler.get('/api/restaurant?name=' +
searchedValue)
            .success(function (data, status, headers,
config) {
                log.debug('Getting restaurants');
                sessionStorage.apiActive = true;
                log.debug("if Restaurants --> " +
restaurantService.restaurants.length);
                if (restaurantService.
orignalRestaurants.length < 1) {
                    restaurantService.
orignalRestaurants = restaurantService.restaurants;
                }
                restaurantService.restaurants = data;
                ajaxHandler.stopSpinner();
                deffered.resolve();
            })
            .error(function (error, status, headers,
config) {
                if (restaurantService.
orignalRestaurants.length < 1) {
                    restaurantService.
orignalRestaurants = restaurantService.restaurants;
                }
                restaurantService.restaurants = [];
                restaurantService.restaurants.push(
                    {
                        id: 104,
                        name: 'Gibsons - Chicago
Rush St.',
                        address: '1028 N. Rush
St., Rush & Division, Cook County, Paris'
                    });
```

```
                            restaurantService.restaurants.push(
                                {
                                    id: 105,
                                    name: 'Harry Caray\'s
Italian Steakhouse',
                                    address: '33 W. Kinzie
St., River North, Cook County, Paris',
                                });
                            ajaxHandler.stopSpinner();
                            deffered.resolve();
                        });
                    return deffered.promise;
                }
            };
            return restaurantService;
        })
```

In the next section of the `restaurants.js` module, we'll add two controllers that we defined for the restaurants and `restaurants.profile` states in the routing configuration. These two controllers are `RestaurantsCtrl` and `RestaurantCtrl` that handle the `restaurants` state and the `restaurants.profiles` states respectively.

`RestaurantsCtrl` is pretty simple in that it loads the restaurants data using the restaurants service list method.

```
        .controller('RestaurantsCtrl', function ($scope,
    restaurantService) {
            $scope.restaurantService = restaurantService;
            restaurantService.async().then(function () {
                $scope.restaurants = restaurantService.list();
            });
        })
```

`RestaurantCtrl` is responsible for showing the restaurant details of a given ID. This is also responsible for performing the reservation operations on the displayed restaurant. This control will be used when we design the restaurant details page with reservation options.

```
        .controller('RestaurantCtrl', function ($scope, $state,
    $stateParams, $injector, restaurantService) {
            var $sessionStorage = $injector.get('$sessionStorage');
            $scope.format = 'dd MMMM yyyy';
            $scope.today = $scope.dt = new Date();
            $scope.dateOptions = {
                formatYear: 'yy',
```

```
                        maxDate: new Date().setDate($scope.today.getDate() +
    180),
                        minDate: $scope.today.getDate(),
                        startingDay: 1
                    };

                    $scope.popup1 = {
                        opened: false
                    };
                    $scope.altInputFormats = ['M!/d!/yyyy'];
                    $scope.open1 = function () {
                        $scope.popup1.opened = true;
                    };
                    $scope.hstep = 1;
                    $scope.mstep = 30;

                    if ($sessionStorage.reservationData) {
                        $scope.restaurant = $sessionStorage.reservationData.
    restaurant;
                        $scope.dt = new Date($sessionStorage.reservationData.
    tm);
                        $scope.tm = $scope.dt;
                    } else {
                        $scope.dt.setDate($scope.today.getDate() + 1);
                        $scope.tm = $scope.dt;
                        $scope.tm.setHours(19);
                        $scope.tm.setMinutes(30);
                        restaurantService.async().then(function () {
                            angular.forEach(restaurantService.list(), function
    (value, key) {
                                if (value.id === parseInt($stateParams.id)) {
                                    $scope.restaurant = value;
                                }
                            });
                        });
                    }
                    $scope.book = function () {
                        var tempHour = $scope.tm.getHours();
                        var tempMinute = $scope.tm.getMinutes();
                        $scope.tm = $scope.dt;
                        $scope.tm.setHours(tempHour);
                        $scope.tm.setMinutes(tempMinute);
                        if ($sessionStorage.currentUser) {
                            console.log("$scope.tm --> " + $scope.tm);
```

```
                    alert("Booking Confirmed!!!");
                    $sessionStorage.reservationData = null;
                    $state.go("restaurants");
                } else {
                    $sessionStorage.reservationData = {};
                    $sessionStorage.reservationData.restaurant =
$scope.restaurant;
                    $sessionStorage.reservationData.tm = $scope.tm;
                    $state.go("login");
                }
            }
        }
    })
```

We have also added a few of the filters in the `restaurants.js` module to format the date and time. These filters perform the following formatting on the input data:

- `date1`: Returns the input date in 'dd MMM yyyy' format, for example 13-Apr-2016

- `time1`: Returns the input time in 'HH:mm:ss' format, for example 11:55:04

- `dateTime1`: Returns the input date and time in 'dd MMM yyyy HH:mm:ss' format, for example 13-Apr-2016 11:55:04

In the following code snippet we've applied these three filters:

```
    .filter('date1', function ($filter) {
        return function (argDate) {
            if (argDate) {
                var d = $filter('date')(new Date(argDate), 'dd MMM
yyyy');
                return d.toString();
            }
            return "";
        };
    })
    .filter('time1', function ($filter) {
        return function (argTime) {
            if (argTime) {
                return $filter('date')(new Date(argTime),
'HH:mm:ss');
            }
            return "";
        };
    })
    .filter('datetime1', function ($filter) {
        return function (argDateTime) {
```

```
                  if (argDateTime) {
                      return $filter('date')(new Date(argDateTime), 'dd
    MMM yyyy HH:mm a');
                  }
                  return "";
              };
          });
```

restaurants.html

We need to add the templates that we have defined for the `restaurants.profile`
state. As you can see in the template we are using the `ng-repeat` directive to
iterate the list of objects returned by `restaurantService.restaurants`. The
`restaurantService` scope variable is defined in the controller. `'RestaurantsCtrl'`
is associated with this template in the restaurants state.

```html
<h3>Famous Gourmet Restaurants in Paris</h3>
<div class="row">
    <div class="col-md-12">
        <table class="table table-bordered table-striped">
            <thead>
                <tr>
                    <th>#Id</th>
                    <th>Name</th>
                    <th>Address</th>
                </tr>
            </thead>
            <tbody>
                <tr ng-repeat="rest in restaurantService.restaurants">
                    <td>{{rest.id}}</td>
                    <td><a ui-sref="restaurants.profile({id: rest.
id})">{{rest.name}}</a></td>
                    <td>{{rest.address}}</td>
                </tr>
            </tbody>
        </table>
    </div>
</div>
```

Search Restaurants

On the home page `index.html` we have added the search form in the `header` section that allows us to search restaurants. The Search Restaurants functionality will use the same files as described earlier. It makes use of the `app.js` (search form handler), `restaurants.js` (restaurant service), and `restaurants.html` to display the searched records.

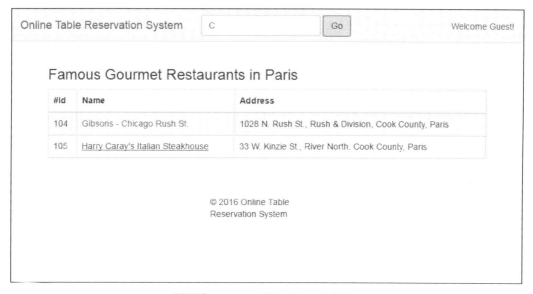

#Id	Name	Address
104	Gibsons - Chicago Rush St.	1028 N. Rush St., Rush & Division, Cook County, Paris
105	Harry Caray's Italian Steakhouse	33 W. Kinzie St., River North, Cook County, Paris

OTRS home page with restaurants listing

Restaurant details with reservation option

Restaurant details with reservation option will be the part of the content area (middle section of the page). This will contain a breadcrumb at the top with restaurants as a link to the restaurant listing page, followed by the name and address of the restaurant. The last section will contain the reservation section containing date time selection boxes and reserve button.

This page will look like the following screenshot:

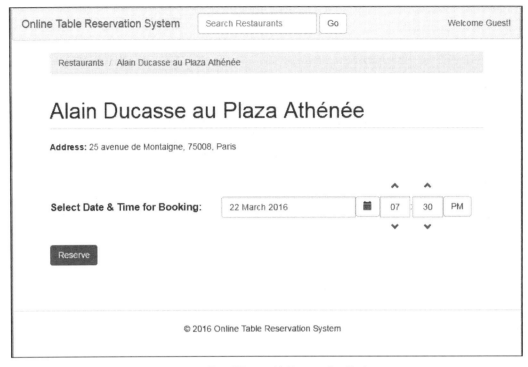

Restaurants Detail Page with Reservation Option

Here, we will make use of the same restaurant service declared in `restaurants.js`. The only change will be the template as described for the state `restaurants.profile`. This template will be defined using the `restaurant.html`.

restaurant.html

As you can see, the breadcrumb is using the restaurants route, which is defined using the `ui-sref` attribute. The reservation form designed in this template calls the `book()` function defined in the controller `RestaurantCtrl` using the directive `ng-submit` on the form submit.

```
<div class="row">
<div class="row">
    <div class="col-md-12">
        <ol class="breadcrumb">
            <li><a ui-sref="restaurants">Restaurants</a></li>
```

```
                  <li class="active">{{restaurant.name}}</li>
          </ol>
          <div class="bs-docs-section">
              <h1 class="page-header">{{restaurant.name}}</h1>
              <div>
                  <strong>Address:</strong> {{restaurant.address}}
              </div>
              </br></br>
              <form ng-submit="book()">
                  <div class="input-append date form_datetime">
                      <div class="row">
                          <div class="col-md-7">
                              <p class="input-group">
                                  <span style="display: table-cell;
vertical-align: middle; font-weight: bolder; font-size: 1.2em">Select
Date & Time for Booking:</span>
                                  <span style="display: table-cell;
vertical-align: middle">
                                      <input type="text" size=20
class="form-control" uib-datepicker-popup="{{format}}" ng-model="dt"
is-open="popup1.opened" datepicker-options="dateOptions" ng-
required="true" close-text="Close" alt-input-formats="altInputFormats"
/>
                                  </span>
                                  <span class="input-group-btn">
                                      <button type="button" class="btn
btn-default" ng-click="open1()"><i class="glyphicon glyphicon
calendar"></i></button>
                                  </span>
                                  <uib-timepicker ng-model="tm" ng-
change="changed()" hour-step="hstep" minute-step="mstep"></uib-
timepicker>
                              </p>
                          </div>
                      </div></div>
                  <div class="form-group">
                      <button class="btn btn-primary"
type="submit">Reserve</button>
                  </div>
              </form></br></br>
          </div>
      </div>
</div>
```

Login page

When a user clicks on the **Reserve** button on the **Restaurant Detail** page after selecting the date and time of the reservation, the **Restaurant Detail** page checks whether the user is already logged in or not. If the user is not logged in, then the **Login** page displays. It looks like the following screenshot:

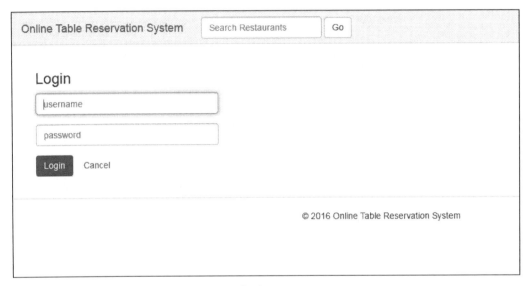

Login page

 We are not authenticating the user from the server. Instead, we are just populating the user name in the session storage and rootscope for implementing the flow.

Once the user logs in, the user is redirected back to same booking page with the persisted state. Then the user can proceed with the reservation. The **Login** page uses basically two files: `login.html` and `login.js`.

login.html

The `login.html` template consists of only two input fields, username and password, with the **Login** button and **Cancel** link. The **Cancel** link resets the form and the **Login** button submits the login form.

Here, we are using the `LoginCtrl` with the `ng-controller` directive. The **Login** form is submitted using the `ng-submit` directive that calls the `submit` function of `LoginCtrl`. Input values are first collected using the `ng-model` directive and then submitted using their respective properties - `_email` and `_password`.

```html
<div ng-controller="LoginCtrl as loginC" style="max-width: 300px">
    <h3>Login</h3>
    <div class="form-container">
        <form ng-submit="loginC.submit(_email, _password)">
            <div class="form-group">
                <label for="username" class="sr-only">Username</label>
                <input type="text" id="username" class="form-control"
placeholder="username" ng-model="_email" required autofocus />
            </div>
            <div class="form-group">
                <label for="password" class="sr-only">Password</label>
                <input type="password" id="password" class="form-
control" placeholder="password" ng-model="_password" />
            </div>
            <div class="form-group">
                <button class="btn btn-primary" type="submit">Login</
button>
                <button class="btn btn-link" ng-click="loginC.
cancel()">Cancel</button>
            </div>
        </form>
    </div>
</div>
```

login.js

The login module is defined in the `login.js` that contains and loads the dependencies using the module function. The state login is defined with the help of the config function that takes the JSON object containing the url, controller, and `templateUrl` properties.

Inside the controller, we define the cancel and submit operations, which are called from the `login.html` template.

```js
angular.module('otrsApp.login', [
    'ui.router',
    'ngStorage'
])
        .config(function config($stateProvider) {
            $stateProvider.state('login', {
```

```
                url: '/login',
                controller: 'LoginCtrl',
                templateUrl: 'login/login.html'
            });
        })
        .controller('LoginCtrl', function ($state, $scope, $rootScope,
$injector) {
            var $sessionStorage = $injector.get('$sessionStorage');
            if ($sessionStorage.currentUser) {
                $state.go($rootScope.fromState.name, $rootScope.
fromStateParams);
            }
            var controller = this;
            var log = $injector.get('$log');
            var http = $injector.get('$http');

            $scope.$on('$destroy', function destroyed() {
                log.debug('LoginCtrl destroyed');
                controller = null;
                $scope = null;
            });
            this.cancel = function () {
                $scope.$dismiss;
                $state.go('restaurants');
            }
            console.log("Current --> " + $state.current);
            this.submit = function (username, password) {
                $rootScope.currentUser = username;
                $sessionStorage.currentUser = username;
                if ($rootScope.fromState.name) {
                    $state.go($rootScope.fromState.name, $rootScope.
fromStateParams);
                } else {
                    $state.go("restaurants");
                }
            };
        });
```

Reservation confirmation

Once the user is logged in and has clicked on the **Reservation** button, the restaurant controller shows the alert box with confirmation as shown in the following screenshot.

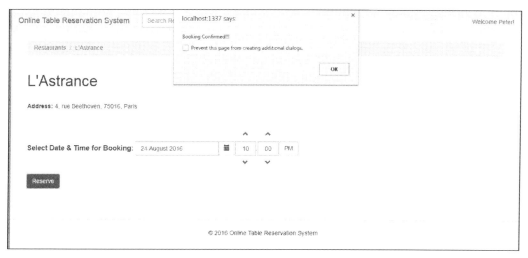

Restaurants detail page with reservation confirmation

Setting up the web app

As we are planning to use the latest technology stack for our UI app development, we will use the Node.js and **npm (Node.js package manager)** that provides the open-source runtime environment for developing the server side JavaScript web application.

I would recommend to go through this section once. It will introduce you to JavaScript build tooling and stack. However, you can skip if you know the JavaScript build tools or do not want to explore them.

Node.js is built on Chrome's V8 JavaScript engine and uses an event-driven, non-blocking I/O, which makes it lightweight and efficient. The default package manager of Node.js, npm, is the largest ecosystem of open source libraries. It allows installing node programs and makes it easier to specify and link dependencies.

1. First we need to install npm if it's not already installed. It is a prerequisite. You can check the link at `https://docs.npmjs.com/getting-started/installing-node` to install npm.

2. To check if npm is set up correctly execute the npm `-v` command on CLI. It should return the installed npm version in the output. We can switch to NetBeans for creating a new AngularJS JS HTML 5 project in NetBeans. At the time of writing this chapter, I have used NetBeans 8.1.

3. Navigate to **File | New Project**. A new project dialog should appear. Select the **HTML5/JavaScript** under the **Categories** list and **HTML5/JS Application** under the **Projects** options as shown in the following screenshot:

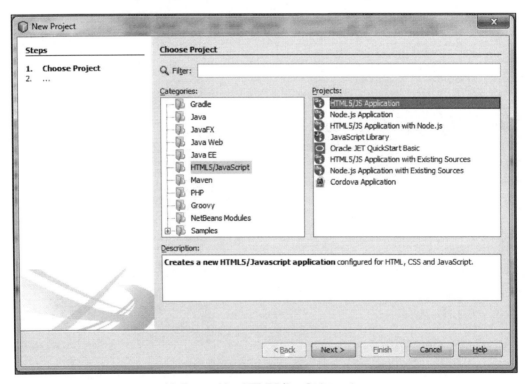

NetBeans – New HTML5/JavaScript project

4. Click on the **Next** button. Then feed the **Project Name, Project Location,** and **Project Folder** on the **Name and Location** dialog and click on the **Next** button.

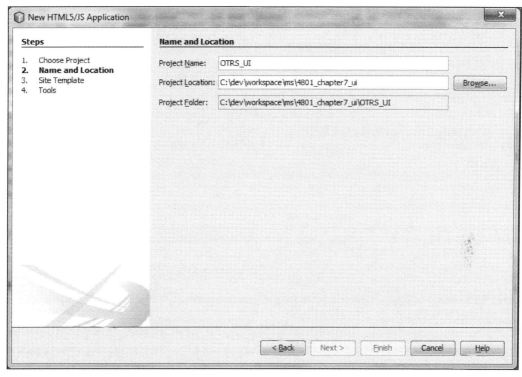

NetBeans New Project – Name and Location

5. On the **Site Template** dialog, select the **AngularJS Seed** item under the **Download Online Template:** option and click on the **Next** button. The AngularJS Seed project is available at `https://github.com/AngularJS/AngularJS-seed`:

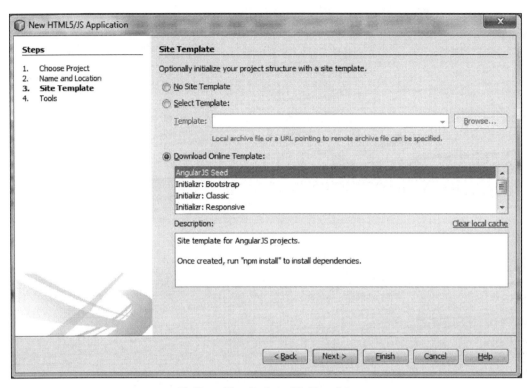

NetBeans New Project – Site Template

6. On the **Tools** dialog, select **Create package.json, Create bower.json**, and **Create gulpfile.js**. We'll use gulp as our build tool. Gulp and Grunt are two of the most popular build framework for JS. As a Java programmer, you can correlate these tools to ANT. Both are awesome in their own way. If you want, you can also use `Gruntfile.js` as a build tool.

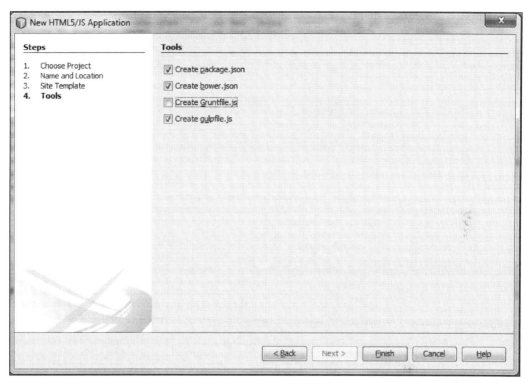

Netbeans New Project - Tools

7. Now, once you click on **Finish**, you can see the HTML5/JS Application directories and files. The directory structure will look like the following screenshot:

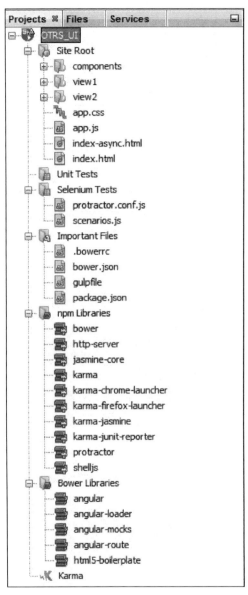

AngularJS seed directory structure

8. You will also see an exclamation mark in your project if all the required dependencies are not configured properly. You can resolve project problems by right clicking the project and then selecting the **Resolve Project Problems** option.

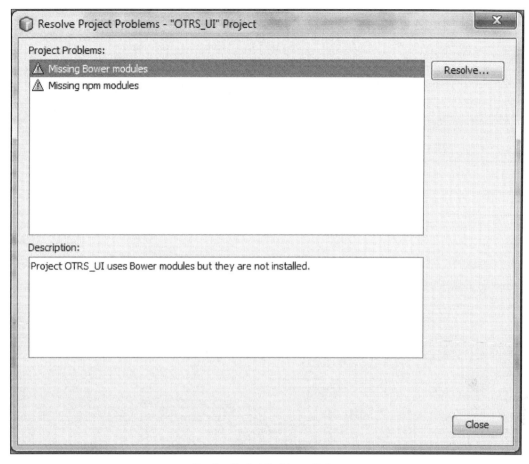

Resolve Project Problems dialog

9. Ideally, NetBeans resolves project problems if you click on the **Resolve...** button.

10. You can also resolve a few of the problems by giving the correct path for some of the JS modules like bower, gulp, and node:

  ○ **Bower**: Required to manage the JavaScript libraries for the OTRS app

  ○ **Gulp**: A task runner, required for building our projects like ANT

  ○ **Node**: For executing our server side OTRS app

Bower is a dependencies management tool that works like npm. npm is used for installing the Node.js modules, whereas bower is used for managing your web application's libraries/components.

11. Click on the **Tools** menu and select **Options**. Now, set the path of bower, gulp, and node.js as shown in the HTML/JS tools (top bar icon) in the following screenshot. For setting up the bower path click on the **Bower** tab as shown in the following screenshot and update the path:

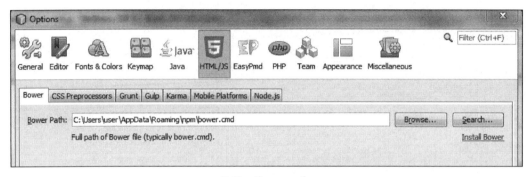

Setting Bower path

12. For setting up the **Gulp Path** click on the **Gulp** tab as shown in the following screenshot and update the path:

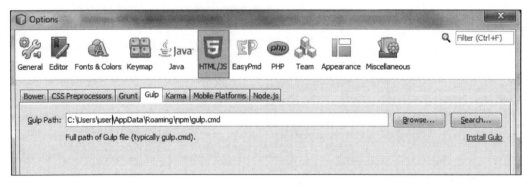

Setting Gulp path

13. For setting up the **Node Path** click on the **Node.js** tab as shown in the following screenshot and update the path:

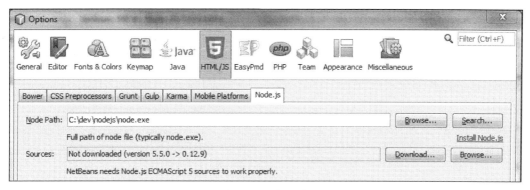

Setting Node path

14. Once this is done, **package.json** will look like the following. We have modified the values for a few of the entries like name, descriptions, dependencies, and so on:

```
{
    "name": "otrs-ui",
    "private": true,
    "version": "1.0.0",
    "description": "Online Table Reservation System",
    "main": "index.js",
    "license": "MIT",
    "dependencies": {
        "coffee-script": "^1.10.0",
        "gulp-AngularJS-templatecache": "^1.8.0",
        "del": "^1.1.1",
        "gulp-connect": "^3.1.0",
        "gulp-file-include": "^0.13.7",
        "gulp-sass": "^2.2.0",
        "gulp-util": "^3.0.7",
        "run-sequence": "^1.1.5"
    },
    "devDependencies": {
        "coffee-script": "*",
        "gulp-sass": "*",
        "bower": "^1.3.1",
        "http-server": "^0.6.1",
        "jasmine-core": "^2.3.4",
        "karma": "~0.12",
        "karma-chrome-launcher": "^0.1.12",
        "karma-firefox-launcher": "^0.1.6",
        "karma-jasmine": "^0.3.5",
        "karma-junit-reporter": "^0.2.2",
```

```
              "protractor": "^2.1.0",
              "shelljs": "^0.2.6"
         },
         "scripts": {
              "postinstall": "bower install",
              "prestart": "npm install",
              "start": "http-server -a localhost -p 8000 -c-1",
              "pretest": "npm install",
              "test": "karma start karma.conf.js",
              "test-single-run": "karma start karma.conf.js  --single-
    run",
              "preupdate-webdriver": "npm install",
              "update-webdriver": "webdriver-manager update",
              "preprotractor": "npm run update-webdriver",
              "protractor": "protractor e2e-tests/protractor.conf.js",
              "update-index-async": "node -e \"require('shelljs/
    global'); sed('-i', /\\/\\/@@NG_LOADER_START@@/,
    [\\s\\S]*\\/\\/@@NG_LOADER_END@@/, '//@@NG_LOADER_
    START@@\\n' + sed(/sourceMappingURL=AngularJS-loader.min.
    js.map/,'sourceMappingURL=bower_components/AngularJS-loader/
    AngularJS-loader.min.js.map','app/bower_components/AngularJS-
    loader/AngularJS-loader.min.js') + '\\n//@@NG_LOADER_END@@', 'app/
    index-async.html');\""
         }
    }
```

15. Then, we'll update the `bower.json` as shown in the following:

```
    {
         "name": "OTRS-UI",
         "description": "OTRS-UI",
         "version": "0.0.1",
         "license": "MIT",
         "private": true,
         "dependencies": {
              "AngularJS": "~1.5.0",
              "AngularJS-ui-router": "~0.2.18",
              "AngularJS-mocks": "~1.5.0",
              "AngularJS-bootstrap": "~1.2.1",
              "AngularJS-touch": "~1.5.0",
              "bootstrap-sass-official": "~3.3.6",
              "AngularJS-route": "~1.5.0",
              "AngularJS-loader": "~1.5.0",
              "ngstorage": "^0.3.10",
              "AngularJS-resource": "^1.5.0",
```

```
        "html5-boilerplate": "~5.2.0"
    }
}
```

16. Next, we'll modify the `.bowerrc` file as shown in the following to specify the directory where bower will store the components defined in `bower.json`. We'll store the bower component under the app directory.

```
{
    "directory": "app/bower_components"
}
```

17. Next, we'll set up the `gulpfile.js`. We'll use `CoffeeScript` to define the gulp tasks. Therefore, we will just define the `CoffeeScript` in `gulpfile.js` and the actual task will be defined in `gulpfile.coffee`. Let's see the content of `gulpfile.js`:

```
require('coffee-script/register');
require('./gulpfile.coffee');
```

18. In this step, we'll define the gulp configuration. We are using `CoffeeScript` to define the gulp file. The name of the `gulp` file written in `CoffeeScript` is `gulpfile.coffee`. The default task is defined as `default_sequence`:

```
default_sequence = ['connect', 'build', 'watch']
```

As per the defined default sequence task, first it will connect to the server, then build the web app, and keep a watch on the changes. The watch will help to render changes we make in the code and will be displayed immediately on the UI.

The most important parts in this script are `connect` and `watch`. Others are self-explanatory.

- ° `gulp-connect`: This is a gulp plugin to run the web server. It also allows live reload.

- ° `gulp-watch`: This is a file watcher that uses chokidar and emits vinyl objects (objects describe the file – its path and content). In simple words, we can say that `gulp-watch` watches files for changes and triggers tasks.

gulpfile.coffee:

```
gulp          = require('gulp')
gutil         = require('gulp-util')
del           = require('del');
clean         = require('gulp-clean')
connect       = require('gulp-connect')
```

```
fileinclude    = require('gulp-file-include')
runSequence    = require('run-sequence')
templateCache  = require('gulp-AngularJS-templatecache')
sass           = require('gulp-sass')

paths =
  scripts:
    src: ['app/src/scripts/**/*.js']
    dest: 'public/scripts'
  scripts2:
    src: ['app/src/views/**/*.js']
    dest: 'public/scripts'
  styles:
    src: ['app/src/styles/**/*.scss']
    dest: 'public/styles'
  fonts:
    src: ['app/src/fonts/**/*']
    dest: 'public/fonts'
  images:
    src: ['app/src/images/**/*']
    dest: 'public/images'
  templates:
    src: ['app/src/views/**/*.html']
    dest: 'public/scripts'
  html:
    src: ['app/src/*.html']
    dest: 'public'
  bower:
    src: ['app/bower_components/**/*']
    dest: 'public/bower_components'

#copy bower modules to public directory
gulp.task 'bower', ->
  gulp.src(paths.bower.src)
  .pipe gulp.dest(paths.bower.dest)
  .pipe connect.reload()

#copy scripts to public directory
gulp.task 'scripts', ->
  gulp.src(paths.scripts.src)
  .pipe gulp.dest(paths.scripts.dest)
  .pipe connect.reload()

#copy scripts2 to public directory
```

```
gulp.task 'scripts2', ->
  gulp.src(paths.scripts2.src)
    .pipe gulp.dest(paths.scripts2.dest)
    .pipe connect.reload()

#copy styles to public directory
gulp.task 'styles', ->
  gulp.src(paths.styles.src)
    .pipe sass()
    .pipe gulp.dest(paths.styles.dest)
    .pipe connect.reload()

#copy images to public directory
gulp.task 'images', ->
  gulp.src(paths.images.src)
    .pipe gulp.dest(paths.images.dest)
    .pipe connect.reload()

#copy fonts to public directory
gulp.task 'fonts', ->
  gulp.src(paths.fonts.src)
    .pipe gulp.dest(paths.fonts.dest)
    .pipe connect.reload()

#copy html to public directory
gulp.task 'html', ->
  gulp.src(paths.html.src)
    .pipe gulp.dest(paths.html.dest)
    .pipe connect.reload()

#compile AngularJS template in a single js file
gulp.task 'templates', ->
  gulp.src(paths.templates.src)
    .pipe(templateCache({standalone: true}))
    .pipe(gulp.dest(paths.templates.dest))

#delete contents from public directory
gulp.task 'clean', (callback) ->
  del ['./public/**/*'], callback;

#Gulp Connect task, deploys the public directory
gulp.task 'connect', ->
  connect.server
    root: ['./public']
```

```
        port: 1337
        livereload: true

    gulp.task 'watch', ->
      gulp.watch paths.scripts.src, ['scripts']
      gulp.watch paths.scripts2.src, ['scripts2']
      gulp.watch paths.styles.src, ['styles']
      gulp.watch paths.fonts.src, ['fonts']
      gulp.watch paths.html.src, ['html']
      gulp.watch paths.images.src, ['images']
      gulp.watch paths.templates.src, ['templates']

    gulp.task 'build', ['bower', 'scripts', 'scripts2', 'styles',
    'fonts', 'images', 'templates', 'html']

    default_sequence = ['connect', 'build', 'watch']

    gulp.task 'default', default_sequence

    gutil.log 'Server started and waiting for changes'
```

19. Once we are ready with the preceding changes, we will install the gulp using the following command:

    ```
    npm install --no-optional gulp
    ```

20. Also, we'll install the other gulp libraries like gulp-clean, gulp-connect, and so on using the following command:

    ```
    npm install --save --no-optional gulp-util gulp-clean gulp-connect
    gulp-file-include run-sequence gulp-AngularJS-templatecache gulp-
    sass
    ```

21. Now, we can install the bower dependencies defined in the bower.json file using the following command:

    ```
    bower install --save
    ```

```
$ bower install --save
bower angular-route#~1.4.0    not-cached git://github.com/angular/bower-angular-route.git#~1.4.0
bower angular-route#~1.4.0        resolve git://github.com/angular/bower-angular-route.git#~1.4.0
bower angular#~1.4.0           not-cached git://github.com/angular/bower-angular.git#~1.4.0
bower angular#~1.4.0               resolve git://github.com/angular/bower-angular.git#~1.4.0
bower angular-loader#~1.4.0   not-cached git://github.com/angular/bower-angular-loader.git#~1.4.0
bower angular-loader#~1.4.0        resolve git://github.com/angular/bower-angular-loader.git#~1.4.0
bower angular-mocks#~1.4.0    not-cached git://github.com/angular/bower-angular-mocks.git#~1.4.0
bower angular-mocks#~1.4.0         resolve git://github.com/angular/bower-angular-mocks.git#~1.4.0
bower html5-boilerplate#~5.2.0      not-cached git://github.com/h5bp/html5-boilerplate.git#~5.2.0
bower html5-boilerplate#~5.2.0         resolve git://github.com/h5bp/html5-boilerplate.git#~5.2.0
bower html5-boilerplate#~5.2.0        download https://github.com/h5bp/html5-boilerplate/archive/5.2.0.tar.gz
bower angular#~1.4.0                  download https://github.com/angular/bower-angular/archive/v1.4.9.tar.gz
bower angular-loader#~1.4.0          download https://github.com/angular/bower-angular-loader/archive/v1.4.9.tar.gz
bower angular-route#~1.4.0           download https://github.com/angular/bower-angular-route/archive/v1.4.9.tar.gz
bower angular-mocks#~1.4.0           download https://github.com/angular/bower-angular-mocks/archive/v1.4.9.tar.gz
bower angular-loader#~1.4.0           extract archive.tar.gz
bower angular-loader#~1.4.0          resolved git://github.com/angular/bower-angular-loader.git#1.4.9
bower html5-boilerplate#~5.2.0        extract archive.tar.gz
bower angular-route#~1.4.0            extract archive.tar.gz
bower angular-route#~1.4.0           resolved git://github.com/angular/bower-angular-route.git#1.4.9
bower html5-boilerplate#~5.2.0    invalid-meta html5-boilerplate is missing "main" entry in bower.json
bower html5-boilerplate#~5.2.0    invalid-meta html5-boilerplate is missing "ignore" entry in bower.json
bower html5-boilerplate#~5.2.0       resolved git://github.com/h5bp/html5-boilerplate.git#5.2.0
bower angular-mocks#~1.4.0            extract archive.tar.gz
bower angular-mocks#~1.4.0           resolved git://github.com/angular/bower-angular-mocks.git#1.4.9
bower angular#~1.4.0                  progress received 0.3MB of 0.5MB downloaded, 53%
bower angular#~1.4.0                  progress received 0.3MB of 0.5MB downloaded, 60%
bower angular#~1.4.0                  progress received 0.4MB of 0.5MB downloaded, 77%
bower angular#~1.4.0                  progress received 0.4MB of 0.5MB downloaded, 88%
bower angular#~1.4.0                  progress received 0.5MB of 0.5MB downloaded, 98%
bower angular#~1.4.0                   extract archive.tar.gz
bower angular#~1.4.0                  resolved git://github.com/angular/bower-angular.git#1.4.9
bower angular-loader#~1.4.0           install angular-loader#1.4.9
bower angular-route#~1.4.0            install angular-route#1.4.9
bower html5-boilerplate#~5.2.0        install html5-boilerplate#5.2.0
bower angular-mocks#~1.4.0            install angular-mocks#1.4.9
bower angular#~1.4.0                   install angular#1.4.9

angular-loader#1.4.9 app\bower_components\angular-loader
└── angular#1.4.9

angular-route#1.4.9 app\bower_components\angular-route
└── angular#1.4.9

html5-boilerplate#5.2.0 app\bower_components\html5-boilerplate

angular-mocks#1.4.9 app\bower_components\angular-mocks
└── angular#1.4.9

angular#1.4.9 app\bower_components\angular
```

Sample output - bower install --save

22. This is the last step in the setup. Here, we will confirm that the directory structure should look like the following. We'll keep the src and published artifacts (in `./public` directory) as separate directories. Therefore, the following directory structure is different from the default AngularJS seed project:

```
+---app
|   +---bower_components
|   |   +---AngularJS
|   |   +---AngularJS-bootstrap
|   |   +---AngularJS-loader
|   |   +---AngularJS-mocks
|   |   +---AngularJS-resource
|   |   +---AngularJS-route
|   |   +---AngularJS-touch
|   |   +---AngularJS-ui-router
|   |   +---bootstrap-sass-official
|   |   +---html5-boilerplate
```

```
|    |    +---jquery
|    |    \---ngstorage
|    +---components
|    |    \---version
|    +---node_modules
|    +---public
|    |    \---css
|    \---src
|         +---scripts
|         +---styles
|         +---views
+---e2e-tests
+---nbproject
|    \---private
+---node_modules
+---public
|    +---bower_components
|    +---scripts
|    +---styles
\---test
```

References to some good reads:

- *AngularJS by Example, Packt Publishing* (https://www.packtpub.com/web-development/angularjs-example)

- *Angular Seed Project* (https://github.com/angular/angular-seed)

- *Angular UI* (https://angular-ui.github.io/bootstrap/)

- *Gulp* (http://gulpjs.com/)

Summary

In this chapter, we have learned the new dynamic web application development. It has changed completely over the years. The web application frontend is completely developed in pure HTML and JavaScript instead of using any server side technologies like JSP, servlets, ASP, and so on. UI app development with JavaScript now has its own development environment like npm, bower, and so on. We have explored the AngularJS framework to develop our web app. It made things easier by providing inbuilt features and support to bootstrap and the $http service that deals with the AJAX calls.

I hope you have grasped the UI development overview and the way modern applications are developed and integrated with server side microservices. In the next chapter, we will learn the best practices and common principals of microservice design. The chapter will provide details about microservices development using industry practices and examples. It will also contain examples of where microservices implementation goes wrong and how you can avoid such problems.

8

Best Practices and Common Principles

After all the hard work put in by you towards gaining the experience of developing the microservice sample project, you must be wondering how to avoid common mistakes and improve the overall process of developing microservices-based products and services. We can follow these principles or guidelines to simplify the process of developing the microservices and avoid/reduce the potential limitations. We will focus on these key concepts in this chapter.

This chapter is spread across the following three sections:

- Overview and mindset
- Best practices and principals
- Microservices frameworks and tools

Overview and mindset

You can implement microservices-based design on both new and existing products and services. Contrary to the belief that it is easier to develop and design a new system from scratch rather than making changes to an existing one that is already live, each approach has its own respective challenges and advantages.

For example, since there is no existing system design for a new product or service, you have freedom and flexibility to design the system without giving any thought to its impact. However, you don't have the clarity on both functional and system requirements for a new system, as these mature and take shape over time. On the other hand, for mature products and services, you have detailed knowledge and information of the functional and system requirements. Nevertheless, you have a challenge to mitigate the risk of impact that design change brings to the table. Therefore, when it comes to updating a production system from monolithic to microservices, you will need to plan better than if you were building a system from scratch.

Experienced and successful software design experts and architects always evaluate the pros and cons and take a cautious approach to making any change to existing live systems. One should not make changes to existing live system design simply because it may be cool or trendy. Therefore, if you would like to update the design of your existing production system to microservices, you need to evaluate all the pros and cons before making this call.

I believe that monolithic systems provide a great platform to upgrade to a successful microservices-based design. Obviously, we are not discussing cost here. You have ample knowledge of the existing system and functionality, which enables you to divide the existing system and build microservices based on functionalities and how those would interact with each other. Also, if your monolithic product is already modularized in some way, then directly transforming microservices by exposing an API instead of **Application Binary Interface (ABI)** is possibly the easiest way of achieving a microservice architecture. A successful microservices-based system is more dependent on microservices and their interaction protocol rather than anything else.

Having said that, it does not mean that you cannot have a successful microservices-based system if you are starting from scratch. However, it is recommended to start a new project based on monolithic design that gives you perspective and understanding of the system and functionality. It allows you to find bottlenecks quickly and guides you to identify any potential feature that can be developed using microservices. Here, we have not discussed the size of the project, which is another important factor. We'll discuss this in the next section.

In today's cloud age and agile development world, it takes an hour between making any change and the change going live. In today's competitive environment, every organization would like to have an edge for quickly delivering features to the user. Continuous development, integration, and deployment are part of the production delivery process, a completely automatic process.

It makes more sense if you are offering cloud-based products or services. Then, a microservices-based system enables the team to respond with agility to fix any issue or provide a new feature to the user.

Therefore, you need to evaluate all pros and cons before you make a call for starting a new microservices-based project from scratch or planning to upgrade the design of an existing monolithic system to a microservices-based system. You have to listen to and understand the different ideas and perspectives shared across your team, and you need to take a cautious approach.

Finally, I would like to share the importance of having better processes and an efficient system in place for a successful production system. Having a microservices-based system does not guarantee a successful production system, and monolithic application does not mean you cannot have a successful production system in today's age. Netflix, a microservices-based cloud video rental service, and Etsy, a monolithic e-commerce platform, are both examples of successful live production systems (see an interesting Twitter discussion link in the *Reference* section later in the chapter). Therefore, processes and agility are also key to a successful production system.

Best practices and principals

As we have learned from the first chapter, microservices are a lightweight style of implementing **Service Oriented Architecture (SOA)**. On top of that, microservices are not strictly defined, which gives you the flexibility of developing microservices the way you want and according to need. At the same time, you need to make sure that you follow a few of the standard practices and principals to make your job easier and implement microservices-based architecture successfully.

Nanoservice (not recommended), size, and monolithic

Each microservice in your project should be small in size and perform one functionality or feature (for example, user management), independently enough to perform the function on its own.

The following two quotes from Mike Gancarz (a member that designed the X windows system), which defines one of the paramount precepts of UNIX philosophy, suits the microservice paradigm as well:

> *"Small is beautiful."*

> *"Make each program do one thing well."*

Now, how to define the size, in today's age, when you have a framework (for example Finangle) that reduces the **lines of code (LOC)**? In addition, many modern languages, such as Python and Erlang, are less verbose. This makes it difficult to decide whether you want to make this code microservice or not.

Apparently, you may implement a microservice for a small number of LOC, that is actually not a microservice but a nanoservice.

Arnon Rotem-Gal-Oz defined nanoservice as follows:

> *"Nanoservice is an antipattern where a service is too fine-grained. A nanoservice is a service whose overhead (communications, maintenance, and so on) outweighs its utility."*

Therefore, it always makes sense to design microservices based on functionality. Domain driven design makes it easier to define functionality at a domain level.

As discussed previously, the size of your project is a key factor when deciding whether to implement microservices or determining the number of microservices you want to have for your project. In a simple and small project, it makes sense to use monolithic architecture. For example, based on the domain design that we learned in *Chapter 3, Domain-Driven Design* you would get a clear understanding of your functional requirements and it makes facts available to draw the boundaries between various functionalities or features. For example, in the sample project (OTRS) we have implemented, it is very easy to develop the same project using monolithic design; provided you don't want to expose the APIs to the customer, or you don't want to use it as SaaS, or there are plenty of similar parameters that you want to evaluate before making a call.

You can migrate the monolithic project to microservices design later, when the need arises. Therefore, it is important that you should develop the monolithic project in modular fashion and have the loose coupling at every level and layer, and ensure there are predefined contact points and boundaries between different functionalities and features. In addition, your data source, such as DB, should be designed accordingly. Even if you are not planning to migrate to a microservices-based system, it would make bug fixes and enhancement easier to implement.

Paying attention to the previous points will mitigate any possible difficulties you may encounter when you migrate to microservices.

Generally, large or complex projects should be developed using microservices-based architecture, due to the many advantages it provides, as discussed in previous chapters.

Even I recommended developing your initial project as monolithic; once you gain a better understanding of project functionalities and project complexity, then you can migrate it to microservices. Ideally, a developed initial prototype should give you the functional boundaries that will enable you to make the right choice.

Continuous integration and deployment

You must have a continuous integration and deployment process in place. It gives you an edge to deliver changes faster and detect bugs early. Therefore, each service should have its own integration and deployment process. In addition, it must be automated. There are many tools available, such as Teamcity, Jenkins, and so on, that are used widely. It helps you to automate the build process — which catches build failure early, especially when you integrate your changes with mainline.

You can also integrate your tests with each automated integration and deployment process. **Integration Testing** tests the interactions of different parts of the system, like between two interfaces (API provider and consumer), or among different components or modules in a system, such as between DAO and database, and so on. Integration testing is important as it tests the interfaces between the modules. Individual modules are first tested in isolation. Then, integration testing is performed to check the combined behavior and validate that requirements are implemented correctly. Therefore, in microservices, integration testing is a key tool to validate the APIs. We will cover more about it in the next section.

Finally, you can see the update mainline changes on your DIT machine where this process deploys the build.

The process does not end here; you can make a container, like docker and hand it over to your WebOps team, or have a separate process that delivers to a configured location or deploy to a WebOps stage environment. From here it could be deployed directly to your production system once approved by the designated authority.

System/end-to-end test automation

Testing is a very important part of any product and service delivery. You do not want to deliver buggy applications to customers. Earlier, at the time when the waterfall model was popular, an organization used to take one to six months or more for the testing stage before delivering to the customer. In recent years, after agile process became popular, more emphasis is given to automation. Similar to prior point testing, automation is also mandatory.

Whether you follow **Test Driven Development** (**TDD**) or not, we must have system or end-to-end test automation in place. It's very important to test your business scenarios and that is also the case with end-to-end testing that may start from your REST call to database checks, or from UI app to database checks.

Also, it is important to test your APIs if you have public APIs.

Doing this makes sure that any change does not break any of the functionality and ensures seamless, bug-free production delivery. As discussed in the last section, each module is tested in isolation using unit testing to check everything is working as expected, then integration testing is performed among different modules to check the expected combined behavior and validate the requirements, whether implemented correctly or not. After integration tests, functional tests are executed that validate the functional and feature requirements.

So, if unit testing makes sure individual modules are working fine in isolation, integration testing makes sure that interaction among different modules works as expected. If unit tests are working fine, it implies that the chances of integration test failure is greatly reduced. Similarly, integration testing ensures that functional testing is likely to be successful.

 It is presumed that one always keeps all types of tests updated, whether these are unit-level tests or end-to-end test scenarios.

Self-monitoring and logging

Microservices should provide service information about itself and the state of the various resources it depends on. Service information represents the statistics such as the average, minimum, and maximum time to process a request, the number of successful and failed requests, being able to track a request, memory usage, and so on.

Adrian Cockcroft highlighted a few practices, which are very important for monitoring the microservices, in **Glue Conference** (**Glue Con**) 2015. Most of them are valid for any monitoring system:

* Spend more time working on code that analyzes the meaning of metrics than code that collects, moves, stores, and displays metrics.

  This helps to not only increase the productivity, but also provides important parameters to fine-tune the microservices and increase the system efficiency. The idea is to develop more analysis tools rather than developing more monitoring tools.

- The metric to display latency needs to be less than the human attention span. That means less than 10 seconds, according to Adrian.

- Validate that your measurement system has enough accuracy and precision. Collect histograms of response time.

- Accurate data makes decision making faster and allows you to fine-tune till precision level. He also suggests that the best graph to show the response time is a histogram.

- Monitoring systems need to be more available and scalable than the systems being monitored.

- The statement says it all: you cannot rely on a system which itself is not stable or available 24/7.

- Optimize for distributed, ephemeral, cloud native, containerized microservices.

- Fit metrics to models to understand relationships.

Monitoring is a key component of microservice architecture. You may have a dozen to thousands of microservices (true for a big enterprise's large project) based on project size. Even for scaling and high availability, organizations create a clustered or load-balanced pool/pod for each microservice, even separate pools for each microservice based on versions. Ultimately, it increases the number of resources you need to monitor, including each microservice instance. In addition, it is important that you should have a process in place so that whenever something goes wrong, you know it immediately, or better, receive a warning notification in advance before something goes wrong. Therefore, effective and efficient monitoring is crucial for building and using the microservice architecture. Netflix uses security monitoring using tools like Netflix Atlas (real-time operational monitoring which processes 1.2 billion metrics), Security Monkey (for monitoring security on AWS-based environments), Scumblr (intelligence gathering tool) and FIDO (for analyzing events and automated incident reporting).

Logging is another important aspect for microservices that should not be ignored. Having effective logging makes all the difference. As there could be 10 or more microservices, managing logging is a huge task.

For our sample project, we have used MDC logging, which is sufficient, in a way, for individual microservice logging. However, we also need logging for an entire system, or central logging. We also need aggregated statistics of logs. There are tools that do the job, like Loggly or Logspout.

A request and generated correlated events gives you an overall view
of the request. For tracing of any event and request, it is important
to associate the event and request with service ID and request ID
respectively. You can also associate the content of the event, such as
message, severity, class name, and so on, to service ID.

A separate data store for each microservice

If you remember, the most important characteristics of microservices you can find
out about is the way microservices run in isolation from other microservices, most
commonly as standalone applications.

Abiding by this rule, it is recommended that you not use the same database, or
any other data store across multiple microservices. In large projects, you may have
different teams working on the same project, and you want the flexibility to choose
the database for each microservice that best suits the microservice.

Now, this also brings some challenges.

For instance, the following is relevant to teams who may be working on different
microservices within the same project, if that project shares the same database
structure. There is a possibility that a change in one microservice may impact the
other microservices model. In such cases, change in one may affect the dependent
microservice, so you also need to change the dependent model structure.

To resolve this issue, microservices should be developed based on an API-driven
platform. Each microservice would expose its APIs, which could be consumed by
the other microservices. Therefore, you also need to develop the APIs, which is
required for the integration of different microservices.

Similarly, due to different data stores, actual project data is also spread across multiple
data stores and it makes data management more complicated, because the separate
storage systems can more easily get out of sync or become inconsistent, and foreign
keys can change unexpectedly. To resolve such an issue, you need to use **Master
Data Management** (**MDM**) tools. MDM tools operate in the background and fix
inconsistencies if they find any. For the OTRS sample example, it might check every
database that stores booking request IDs, to verify that the same IDs exist in all of
them (in other words, that there aren't any missing or extra IDs in any one database).
MDM tools available in the market include Informatica, IBM MDM Advance Edition,
Oracle Siebel UCM, Postgres (master streaming replication), mariadb (master/master
configuration), and so on.

If none of the existing products suit your requirements, or you are not interested in any proprietary product, then you can write your own. Presently, API-driven development and platform reduce such complexities; therefore, it is important that microservices should be developed along with an API platform.

Transaction boundaries

We have gone through domain driven design concepts in *Chapter 3, Domain-Driven Design*. Please review this if you have not grasped it thoroughly, as it gives you an understanding of the state vertically. Since we are focusing on microservices-based design, the result is that we have a system of systems, where each microservice represents a system. In this environment, finding the state of a whole system at any given point in time is very challenging. If you are familiar with distributed applications, then you may be comfortable in such an environment, with respect to state.

It is very important to have transaction boundaries in place that describe which microservice owns a message at any given time. You need a way or process that can participate in transactions, transacted routes and error handlers, idempotent consumers, and compensating actions. It is not an easy task to ensure transactional behavior across heterogeneous systems, but there are tools available that do the job for you.

For example, Camel has great transactional capabilities that help developers easily create services with transactional behavior.

Microservices frameworks and tools

It is always better not to reinvent the wheel. Therefore, we would like to explore what tools are already available and provide the platform, framework, and features that make microservices development and deployment easier.

Throughout the book, we have used the Spring Cloud extensively, due to the same reason; it provides all the tools and platform required to make microservice development very easy. Spring Cloud uses the Netflix **Open Source Software (OSS)**. Let us explore Netflix OSS—a complete package.

I have also added a brief overview about how each tool will help to build good microservice architecture.

Netflix Open Source Software (OSS)

Netflix OSS center is the most popular and widely-used open source software for Java-based microservice open source projects. The world's most successful video renting service is dependent on it. Netflix has more than 40 million users and is used across the globe. Netflix is a pure cloud-based solution, developed on microservice-based architecture. You can say that whenever anybody talks about microservices, Netflix is the first name that comes to mind. Let us discuss the wide variety of tools it provides. We have already discussed many of them while developing the sample OTRS app. However, there are a few which we have not explored. Here, we'll cover only the overview of each tool, instead of going into detail. It will give you an overall idea of the practical characteristics of microservices architecture and its use in Cloud.

Build – Nebula

Netflix Nebula is a collection of Gradle plugins that makes your microservice builds easier using Gradle (a Maven-like build tool). For our sample project, we have made use of Maven, therefore we haven't had the opportunity to explore Nebula in this book. However, exploring it would be fun. The most significant Nebula feature for developers is eliminating the boilerplate code in Gradle build files, which allows developers to focus on coding.

> Having a good build environment, especially CI/CD (continuous integration and continuous deployment) is a must for microservice development and keeping aligned with agile development. Netflix Nebula makes your build easier and more efficient.

Deployment and delivery – Spinnaker with Aminator

Once your build is ready, you want to move that build to **Amazon Web Services (AWS)** EC2. Aminator creates and packages images of builds in the form of **Amazon Machine Image (AMI)**. Spinnaker then deploys these AMIs to AWS.

Spinnaker is a continuous delivery platform for releasing code changes with high velocity and efficiency. Spinnaker also supports other cloud services, such as Google Computer Engine and Cloud Foundry.

> You would like to deploy your latest microservice builds to cloud environments like EC2. Spinnaker and Aminator helps you to do that in an autonomous way.

Service registration and discovery – Eureka

Eureka, as we have explored in this book provides a service that is responsible for microservice registration and discovery. On top of that, Eureka is also used for load-balancing the middle-tier (processes hosting different microservices). Netflix also uses Eureka, along with other tools, like Cassandra or memcached, to enhance its overall usability.

 Service registration and discovery is a must for microservice architecture. Eureka serves this purpose. Please refer to *Chapter 4, Implementing Microservices* for more information about Eureka.

Service communication – Ribbon

Microservice architecture is of no use if there is no inter-process or service communication. The Ribbon application provides this feature. Ribbon works with Eureka for load balancing and with Hystrix for fault tolerance or circuit breaker operations.

Ribbon also supports TCP and UDP protocols, apart from HTTP. It provides these protocol supports in both asynchronous and reactive models. It also provides the caching and batching capabilities.

 Since you will have many microservices in your project, you need a way to process information using inter-process or service communication. Netflix provides the Ribbon tool for this purpose.

Circuit breaker – Hystrix

Hystrix tool is for circuit breaker operations, that is, latency and fault tolerance. Therefore, Hystrix stops cascading failures. Hystrix performs the real-time operations for monitoring the services and property changes, and supports concurrency.

 Circuit breaker, or fault tolerance, is an important concept for any project, including microservices. Failure of one microservice should not halt your entire system; to prevent this, and provide meaningful information to the customer on failure, is the job of Netflix Hystrix.

Edge (proxy) server – Zuul

Zuul is an edge server or proxy server, and serves the requests of external applications such as UI client, Android/iOS app, or any third-party consumer of APIs offered by the product or service. Conceptually, it is a door to external applications.

Zuul allows dynamic routing and monitoring of requests. It also performs security operations like authentication. It can identify authentication requirements for each resource and reject any request that does not satisfy them.

> You need an edge server or API gateway for your microservices. Netflix Zuul provides this feature. Please refer to *Chapter 5, Deployment and Testing* for more information.

Operational monitoring – Atlas

Atlas is an operational monitoring tool that provides near real-time information on dimensional time-series data. It captures operational intelligence that provides a picture of what is currently happening within a system. It features in-memory data storage, allowing it to gather and report very large numbers of metrics very quickly. At present, it processes 1.3 billion metrics for Netflix.

Atlas is a scalable tool. This is why it can now process 1.3 billion metrics, from 1 million metrics a few years back. Atlas not only provides scalability in terms of reading the data, but also aggregating it as a part of graph request.

Atlas uses the Netflix Spectator library for recording dimensional time-series data.

> Once you deploy microservices in Cloud environment, you need to have a monitoring system in place to track and monitor all microservices. Netflix Atlas does this job for you

Reliability monitoring service – Simian Army

In Cloud, no single component can guarantee 100% uptime. Therefore, it is a requirement for successful microservice architecture to make the entire system available in case a single cloud component fails. Netflix has developed a tool named Simian Army to avoid system failure. Simian Army keeps a cloud environment safe, secure, and highly available. To achieve high availability and security, it uses various services (Monkeys) in the cloud for generating various kinds of failures, detecting abnormal conditions, and testing the cloud's ability to survive these challenges. It uses the following services (Monkeys), which are taken from the Netflix blog:

- **Chaos Monkey**: Chaos Monkey is a service which identifies groups of systems and randomly terminates one of the systems in a group. The service operates at a controlled time and interval. Chaos Monkey only runs in business hours with the intent that engineers will be alert and able to respond.

- **Janitor Monkey**: Janitor Monkey is a service which runs in the AWS cloud looking for unused resources to clean up. It can be extended to work with other cloud providers and cloud resources. The schedule of service is configurable. Janitor Monkey determines whether a resource should be a cleanup candidate, by applying a set of rules on it. If any of the rules determines that the resource is a cleanup candidate, Janitor Monkey marks the resource and schedules a time to clean it up. For exceptional cases, when you want to keep an unused resource longer, before Janitor Monkey deletes a resource, the owner of the resource will receive a notification a configurable number of days ahead of the cleanup time.

- **Conformity Monkey**: Conformity Monkey is a service which runs in the AWS cloud looking for instances that are not conforming to predefined rules for the best practices. It can be extended to work with other cloud providers and cloud resources. The schedule of service is configurable.

  If any of the rules determines that the instance is not conforming, the monkey sends an e-mail notification to the owner of the instance. There could be exceptional cases where you want to ignore warnings of a specific conformity rule for some applications.

- **Security Monkey**: Security Monkey monitors policy changes and alerts on insecure configurations in an AWS account. The main purpose of Security Monkey is security, though it also proves a useful tool for tracking down potential problems, as it is essentially a change-tracking system.

- Successful microservice architecture makes sure that your system is always up, and failure of a single cloud component should not fail the entire system. Simian Army uses many services to achieve high availability.

AWS resource monitoring – Edda

In a cloud environment, nothing is static. For example, virtual host instance changes frequently, an IP address could be reused by various applications, or a firewall or related changes may take place.

Edda is a service that keeps track of these dynamic AWS resources. Netflix named it Edda (meaning *a tale of Norse mythology*), as it records the tales of cloud management and deployments. Edda uses the AWS APIs to poll AWS resources and records the results. These records allow you to search and see how the cloud has changed over time. For instance, if any host of the API server is causing any issue, then you need to find out what that host is and which team is responsible for it.

These are the features it offers:

- **Dynamic querying**: Edda provides the REST APIs, and it supports the matrix arguments and provides fields selectors that let you retrieve only the desired data.

- **History/Changes**: Edda maintains the history of all AWS resources. This information helps you when you analyze the causes and impact of outage. Edda can also provide the different view of current and historical information about resources. It stores the information in MongoDB at the time of writing.

- **Configuration**: Edda supports many configuration options. In general, you can poll information from multiple accounts and multiple regions and can use the combination of account and regions that account points. Similarly, it provides different configurations for AWS, Crawler, Elector, and MongoDB.

- If you are using the AWS for hosting your microservice based product, then Edda serves the purpose of monitoring the AWS resources.

On-host performance monitoring – Vector

Vector is a static web application and runs inside a web browser. It allows it to monitor the performance of those hosts where **Performance Co-Pilot (PCP)** is installed. Vector supports PCP version 3.10+. PCP collects metrics and makes them available to Vector.

It provides high-resolution right metrics available on demand. This helps engineers to understand how a system behaves and correctly troubleshoot performance issues.

 A monitoring tool that helps you to monitor the performance of a remote host.

Distributed configuration management – Archaius

Archaius is a distributed configuration management tool that allows you to do the following:

- Use dynamic and typed properties
- Perform thread-safe configuration operations
- Check for property changes using a polling framework
- Use a callback mechanism in an ordered hierarchy of configurations
- Inspect and perform operations on properties using JConsole, as Archaius provides the JMX MBean
- A good configuration management tool is required when you have a microservices-based product. Archaius helps to configure different types of properties in a distributed environment.

Scheduler for Apache Mesos – Fenzo

Fenzo is a scheduler library for Apache Mesos frameworks written in Java. Apache Mesos frameworks match and assign resources to pending tasks. The following are its key features:

- It supports long-running service style tasks and for batch
- It can auto-scale the execution host cluster, based on resource demands
- It supports plugins that you can create based on requirements
- You can monitor resource-allocation failures, which allows you to debug the root cause

Cost and cloud utilization – Ice

Ice provides a bird's eye view of cloud resources from a cost and usage perspective. It provides the latest information of provisioned cloud resources allocation to different teams that add value for optimal utilization of the cloud resources.

Ice is a grail project. Users interacts with the Ice UI component that displays the information sent via the Ice reader component. The reader fetches information from the data generated by the Ice processor component. The Ice processor component reads data information from a detailed cloud billing file and converts it into data that is readable by the Ice reader component.

Other security tools – Scumblr and FIDO

Along with Security Monkey, Netflix OSS also makes use of Scumblr and **Fully Integrated Defense Operation (FIDO)** tools.

 To keep track and protect your microservices from regular threats and attacks, you need an automated way to secure and monitor your microservices. Netflix Scumblr and FIDO do this job for you.

Scumblr

Scumblr is a Ruby on Rails-based web application that allows you to perform periodic searches and store/take action on the identified results. Basically, it gathers intelligence that leverages Internet-wide targeted searches to surface specific security issues for investigation.

Scumblr makes use of Workflowable gem to allow setting up flexible workflows for different types of results. Scumblr searches utilize plugins called **Search Providers**. It checks the anomaly like following. Since it is extensible, you can add as many as you want:

- Compromised credentials
- Vulnerability/hacking discussion
- Attack discussion
- Security-relevant social media discussion

Fully Integrated Defence Operation (FIDO)

FIDO is a security orchestration framework for analyzing events and automating incident responses. It automates the incident response process by evaluating, assessing and responding to malware. FIDO's primary purpose is to handle the heavy manual effort needed to evaluate threats coming from today's security stack and the large number of alerts generated by them.

As an orchestration platform, FIDO can make using your existing security tools more efficient and accurate by heavily reducing the manual effort needed to detect, notify, and respond to attacks against a network. For more information, you can refer these following links:

```
https://github.com/Netflix/Fido  https://github.com/Netflix
```

References

- Monolithic (Etsy) versus Microservices (Netflix) Twitter discussion
  `https://twitter.com/adrianco/status/441169921863860225`

- *Monitoring Microservice and Containers Presentation* by Adrian Cockcroft:
  `http://www.slideshare.net/adriancockcroft/gluecon-monitoring-microservices-and-containers-a-challenge`

- Nanoservice Antipattern: `http://arnon.me/2014/03/services-microservices-nanoservices/`

- Apache Camel for Microservice Architectures: `https://www.javacodegeeks.com/2014/09/apache-camel-for-micro%C2%ADservice-architectures.html`

- Teamcity: `https://www.jetbrains.com/teamcity/`

- Jenkins: `https://jenkins-ci.org/`

- Loggly: `https://www.loggly.com/`

Summary

In this chapter, we have explored various practices and principles, which are best-suited for microservices-based products and services. Microservices architecture is a result of cloud environments, which are being used widely in comparison to on-premise-based monolithic systems. We have identified a few of the principals related to size, agility, and testing, that have to be in place for successful implementation.

We have also got an overview of different tools used by Netflix OSS for the various key features required for successful implementation of microservices architecture-based products and services. Netflix offers a video rental service, using the same tools successfully.

In the next chapter, readers may encounter issues and they may get stuck at those problems. The chapter explains the common problems encountered during the development of microservices, and their solutions.

9
Troubleshooting Guide

We have come so far and I am sure you are enjoying each and every moment of this challenging and joyful learning journey. I will not say that this book ends after this chapter, but rather you are completing the first milestone. This milestone opens the doors for learning and implementing a new paradigm in the cloud with microservice-based design. I would like to reaffirm that integration testing is an important way to test interaction among microservices and APIs. While working on your sample app **Online Table Reservation System** (**OTRS**), I am sure you faced many challenges, especially while debugging the app. Here, we will cover a few of the practices and tools that will help you to troubleshoot the deployed application, Docker containers, and host machines.

This chapter covers the following three topics:

- Logging and ELK stack
- Use of correlation ID for service calls
- Dependencies and versions

Logging and ELK stack

Can you imagine debugging any issue without seeing a log on the production system? Simply, no, as it would be difficult to go back in time. Therefore, we need logging. Logs also give us warning signals about the system if they are designed and coded that way. Logging and log analysis is an important step for troubleshooting any issue, and also for throughput, capacity, and monitoring the health of the system. Therefore, having a very good logging platform and strategy will enable effective debugging. Logging is one of the most important key components of software development in the initial days.

Microservices are generally deployed using image containers like Docker that provide the log with commands that help you to read logs of services deployed inside the containers. Docker and Docker Compose provide commands to stream the log output of running services within the container and in all containers respectively. Please refer to the following `logs` command of Docker and Docker Compose:

Docker logs command:

Usage: `docker logs [OPTIONS] <CONTAINER NAME>`

```
Fetch the logs of a container:
  -f, --follow      Follow log output
  --help       Print usage
  --since=""                   Show logs since
timestamp
  -t, --timestamps             Show timestamps
  --tail="all"                 Number of lines to show
from the end of the logs
```

Docker Compose logs Command:

`Usage: docker-compose logs [options] [SERVICE...]`

Options:

```
--no-color  Produce monochrome output
-f, --follow  Follow log output
-t, --timestamps  Show timestamps
--tail     Number of lines to show from the end of the
logs for each  container
[SERVICES...]  Service representing the container - you
can give multiple
```

These commands help you to explore the logs of microservices and other processes running inside the containers. As you can see, using the above commands would be a challenging task when you have a higher number of services. For example, if you have 10s or 100s of microservices, it would be very difficult to track each microservice log. Similarly, you can imagine, even without containers, how difficult it would be to monitor logs individually. Therefore, you can assume the difficulty of exploring and correlating the logs of 10s to 100s of containers. It is time-consuming and adds very little value.

Therefore, a log aggregator and visualizing tools like the ELK stack come to our rescue. It will be used for centralizing logging. We'll explore this in the next section.

A brief overview

The **Elasticsearch, Logstash, Kibana** (**ELK**) stack is a chain of tools that performs log aggregation, analysis, visualization, and monitoring. The ELK stack provides a complete logging platform that allows you to analyze, visualize, and monitor all your logs, including all types of product logs and system logs. If you already know about the ELK stack, please skip to the next section. Here, we'll provide a brief introduction to each tool in the ELK Stack.

Elasticsearch

Elasticsearch is one of the most popular enterprise full text search engines. It is open sourced software. It is distributable and supports multitenancy. A single Elasticsearch server stores multiple indexes (each index represents a database), and a single query can search data of multiple indexes. It is a distributed search engine and supports clustering.

It is readily scalable and can provide near real-time searches with a latency of 1 second. It is developed in Java using Apache Lucene. Apache Lucene is also free, open sourced, and it provides the core of Elasticsearch, aka the informational retrieval software library.

Elasticsearch APIs are extensive in nature and very elaborative. Elasticsearch provides a JSON-based schema, less storage, and represents data models in JSON. Elasticsearch APIs use JSON documents for HTTP requests and responses.

Logstash

Logstash is an open source data collection engine with real-time pipeline capabilities. In simple words, it collects, parses, processes, and stores the data. Since Logstash has data pipeline capabilities, helping you to process any event data, like logs, from a variety of systems. Logstash runs as an agent that collects the data, parses it, filters it, and sends the output to a designated app, such as Elasticsearch, or simple standard output on a console.

It is also has a very good plugin ecosystem (image sourced from `www.elastic.co`):

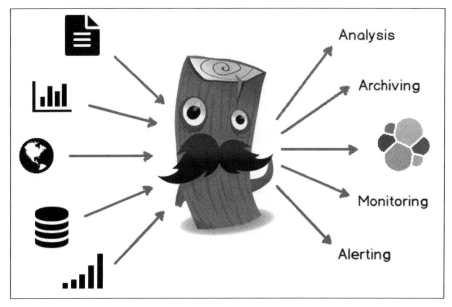

Logstash ecosystem

Kibana

Kibana is an open source analytics and visualization web application. It is designed to work with Elasticsearch. You use Kibana to search, view, and interact with data stored in Elasticsearch indices.

It is a browser-based web application that lets you perform advanced data analysis and visualize your data in a variety of charts, tables, and maps. Moreover, it is a zero-configuration application. Therefore, it neither needs any coding nor additional infrastructure after installation.

ELK stack setup

Generally, these tools are installed individually and then configured to communicate with each other. The installation of these components is pretty straight forward. Download the installable artifact from the designated location and follow the installation steps as shown in the next section.

The installation steps provided below are part of a basic setup, which is required for setting up the ELK stack you want to run. Since this installation was done on my localhost machine, I have used the host localhost. It can be changed easily with any respective host name that you want.

Installing Elasticsearch

We can install Elasticsearch by following these steps:

1. Download the latest Elasticsearch distribution from `https://www.elastic.co/downloads/elasticsearch`.

2. Unzip it to the desired location in your system.

3. Make sure the latest Java version is installed and the `JAVA_HOME` environment variable is set.

4. Go to Elasticsearch home and run `bin/elasticsearch` on Unix-based systems and `bin/elasticsearch.bat` on Windows.

5. Open any browser and hit `http://localhost:9200/`. On successful installation it should provide you a JSON object similar to that shown as follows:

    ```
    {
      "name" : "Leech",
      "cluster_name" : "elasticsearch",
      "version" : {
        "number" : "2.3.1",
        "build_hash" : "bd980929010aef404e7cb0843e61d0665269fc39",
        "build_timestamp" : "2016-04-04T12:25:05Z",
        "build_snapshot" : false,
        "lucene_version" : "5.5.0"
      },
      "tagline" : "You Know, for Search"
    }
    ```

    By default, the GUI is not installed. You can install one by executing the following command from the `bin` directory; make sure the system is connected to the Internet:

    ```
    plugin -install mobz/elasticsearch-head
    ```

6. Now you can access the GUI interface with the URL `http://localhost:9200/_plugin/head/`.

    You can replace `localhost` and `9200` with your respective hostname and port number.

Installing Logstash

We can install Logstash by following the given steps:

1. Download the latest Logstash distribution from `https://www.elastic.co/downloads/logstash`.

2. Unzip it to the desired location in your system.

    Prepare a configuration file, as shown below. It instructs Logstash to read input from given files and passes it to Elasticsearch (see the following `config` file; Elasticsearch is represented by localhost and `9200` port). It is the simplest configuration file. To add filters and learn more about Logstash, you can explore the Logstash reference documentation available at `https://www.elastic.co/guide/en/logstash/current/index.html`.

> As you can see, the OTRS `service` log and `edge-server` log are added as input. Similarly, you can also add log files of other microservices.

```
input {
  ### OTRS ###
  file {
    path => "\logs\otrs-service.log"
    type => "otrs-api"
    codec => "json"
    start_position => "beginning"
  }

  ### edge ###
  file {
    path => "/logs/edge-server.log"
    type => "edge-server"
    codec => "json"
  }
}

output {
  stdout {
    codec => rubydebug
  }
  elasticsearch {
    hosts => "localhost:9200"
  }
}
```

3. Go to Logstash home and run `bin/logstash agent -f logstash.conf` on Unix-based systems and `bin/logstash.bat agent -f logstash.conf` on Windows. Here, Logstash is executed using the `agent` command. Logstash agent collects data from the sources provided in the input field in the configuration file and sends the output to Elasticsearch. Here, we have not used the filters, because otherwise it may process the input data before providing it to Elasticsearch.

Installing Kibana

We can install the Kibana web application by following the given steps:

1. Download the latest Kibana distribution from `https://www.elastic.co/downloads/kibana`.

2. Unzip it to the desired location in your system.

3. Open the configuration file `config/kibana.yml` from the Kibana home directory and point the `elasticsearch.url` to the previously configured Elasticsearch instance:

   ```
   elasticsearch.url: "http://localhost:9200"
   ```

4. Go to Kibana home and run `bin/kibana agent -f logstash.conf` on Unix-based systems and `bin/kibana.bat agent -f logstash.conf` on Windows.

5. Now you can access the Kibana app from your browser using the URL `http://localhost:5601/`.

   To learn more about Kibana, explore the Kibana reference documentation at `https://www.elastic.co/guide/en/kibana/current/getting-started.html`.

As we followed the above steps, you may have noticed that it requires some amount of effort. If you want to avoid a manual setup, you can Dockerize it. If you don't want to put effort into creating the Docker container of the ELK stack, you can choose one from Docker Hub. On Docker Hub there are many ready-made ELK stack Docker images. You can try different ELK containers and choose the one that suits you the most. willdurand/elk is the most downloaded container and is easy to start, working well with Docker Compose.

Tips for ELK stack implementation

- To avoid any data loss and handle the sudden spike of input load, using a broker, such as Redis or RabbitMQ, is recommended between Logstash and Elasticsearch.

- Use an odd number of nodes for Elasticsearch if you are using clustering to prevent the split-brain problem.

- In Elasticsearch, always use the appropriate field type for given data. This will allow you to perform different checks, for example, the `int` field type will allow you to perform (`"http_status: <400"`) or (`"http_status:=200"`). Similarly, other field types also allow you to perform similar checks.

Use of correlation ID for service calls

When you make a call to any REST endpoint and if any issue pops up, it is difficult to trace the issue and its root origin because each call is made to server, and this call may call another and so on and so forth. This makes it very difficult to figure out how one particular request was transformed and what it was called. Normally, an issue that is caused by one service can cause service elsewhere. It is very difficult to track and may require an enormous amount of effort. If it is monolithic, you know that you are looking in the right direction but microservices make it difficult to understand what the source of the issue is and where you should get your data.

Let's see how we can tackle this problem

By using a correlation ID that is passed across all calls, it allows you to track each request and track the route easily. Each request will have its unique correlation ID. Therefore, when we debug any issue, the correlation ID is our starting point. We can follow it, and along the way, we can find out what went wrong.

The correlation ID requires some extra development effort, but it's effort well spent as it helps a lot in the long run. When a request travels between different microservices, you will be able to see all interactions and which service has problems.

This is not something new or invented for microservices. This pattern is already being used by many popular products such as Microsoft SharePoint.

Dependencies and versions

Two common problems that we face in product development are cyclic dependencies and API versions. We'll discuss them in terms of microservice based architectures.

Cyclic dependencies and their impact

Generally, monolithic architecture has a typical layer model, whereas microservices carry the graph model. Therefore, microservices may have cyclic dependencies.

Therefore, it is necessary to keep a dependency check on microservice relationships.

Let us have a look at the following two cases:

- If you have a cycle of dependencies between your microservices, you are vulnerable to distributed stack overflow errors when a certain transaction might be stuck in a loop. For example, when a restaurant table is being reserved by a person. In this case, the restaurant needs to know the person (findBookedUser), and the person needs to know the restaurant at a given time (findBookedRestaurant). If it is not designed well, these services may call each other in loop. The result may be a stack overflow generated by JVM.

- If two services share a dependency and you update that other service's API in a way that could affect them, you'll need to updated all three at once. This brings up questions like, which should you update first? In addition, how do you make this a safe transition?

It needs to be analyzed while designing the system

Therefore, it is important while designing the microservices to establish the proper relationship between different services internally to avoid any cyclic dependencies. It is a design issue and must be addressed even if it requires a refactoring of the code.

Maintaining different versions

When you have more services, it means different release cycles for each of them, which adds to this complexity by introducing different versions of services, in that there will be different versions of the same REST services. Reproducing the solution to a problem will prove to be very difficult when it has gone in one version and returns in a newer one.

Let's explore more

The versioning of APIs is important because with time APIs change. Your knowledge and experience improves with time, and that leads to changes in APIs. Changing APIs may break existing client integrations.

Therefore, there are various ways for managing the API versions. One of these is using the version in the path that we have used in this book; some also use the HTTP header. The HTTP header could be a custom request header or you could use the *Accept Header* for representing the calling API version. For more information on how versions are handled using HTTP headers, please refer to *RESTful Java Patterns and Best Practices* by Bhakti Mehta, Packt Publishing: `https://www.packtpub.com/application-development/restful-java-patterns-and-best-practices`.

It is very important while troubleshooting any issue that your microservices are implemented to produce the version numbers in logs. In addition, ideally, you should avoid any instance where you have too many versions of any microservice.

References

This following links will have more information:

- Elasticsearch: `https://www.elastic.co/products/elasticsearch`
- Logstash: `https://www.elastic.co/products/logstash`
- Kibana: `https://www.elastic.co/products/kibana`
- `willdurand/elk`: ELK Docker image
- *Mastering Elasticsearch – Second Edition*: `https://www.packtpub.com/web-development/mastering-elasticsearch-second-edition`

Summary

In this chapter, we have explored the ELK stack overview and installation. In the ELK stack, Elasticsearch is used for storing the logs and service queries from Kibana. Logstash is an agent that runs on each server that you wish to collect logs from. Logstash reads the logs, filters/transforms them, and provides them to Elasticsearch. Kibana reads/queries the data from Elasticsearch and presents it in tabular or graphical visualizations.

We also understand the utility of having the correlation ID while debugging issues. At the end of this chapter, we also discovered the shortcomings of a few microservice designs. It was a challenging task to cover all the topics relating to microservices in this book, so I tried to include as much relevant information as possible with precise sections with references, which allow you to explore more. Now I would like to let you start implementing the concepts we have learned in this chapter to your workplace or in your personal projects. This will not only give you hands-on experience, but may also allow you to master microservices. In addition, you will also be able to participate in local meetups and conferences.

Index

Symbol

μService
  booking 86
  developing 73
  discovery service (Eureka service) 86, 87
  entities 73
  evolution 2
  execution 88
  implementing 73
  Maven dependency 86
  monolithic architecture overview 3
  registration 86, 87
  Repository object 73, 74
  Restaurant μService 74, 75
  services 73
  spring configurations 87
  startup class 87
  used, for specifying limitations of
      monolithic architecture versus
      solution 3-6
  user services 86

A

**Advance Messaging Queue Protocol
      (AMQP) 105**
Amazon Machine Image (AMI) 214
Amazon Web Services (AWS) 214
Aminator 214
AngularJS framework
  controllers 163
  directives 164
  filters 164

  modules 161, 162
  MVC (Model View Controller) 160
  MVVM (Model-View-ViewModel) 160
  overview 160
  providers 162, 163
  scopes 163
  services 162, 163
  UI-Router 164, 165
AngularJS module
  config() 162
  run() 162
API versions
  about 230
  exploring 231, 232
  references 232
App class 87
Application Binary Interface (ABI) 206
application build, setting up
  about 29
  execution, Java command used 30
  Maven tool, running 29, 30
Archaius 219
artifacts, domain-driven design (DDD)
  aggregates 51, 52
  entities 47
  factory 54
  modules 56
  repository 53
  services 50
  value objects (VOs) 48
Atlas 216
authentication
  OAuth 2.0 126
  providing 125

authorization
  OAuth 2.0 126
  providing 125
authorization code grant, OAuth 2.0
        grant types
  about 136
  code requests and responses 136-140

B

best practices and principals
  about 207
  continuous integration 209
  deployment 209
  logging 210, 211
  monolithic 207, 208
  nanoservice 207, 208
  self-monitoring 210, 211
  separate data store, for microservice 212
  size 207, 208
  system/end-to-end test
        automation 209, 210
  transaction boundaries 213
building blocks, domain-driven design
        (DDD)
  about 45
  multilayered architecture 45
  ubiquitous language 45

C

CalculationController 26
Certificate Authority (CA) 122
circuit breaker
  about 102
  Hystrix Dashboard, setting up 105, 106
  Hystrix's fallback methods,
        implementing 102, 103
  monitoring 102-105
  Turbine, setting up 107, 108
client-side load balancing
  about 95, 96
  DiscoveryClient sample 97
  features 95
  FeignClient sample 98
  RESTTemplate sample 97

client types, OAuth 2.0 client registration
  about 130
  confidential 130
  native application 132
  public 130
  user agent-based application 132
  web application 131
common name (CN) 124
container
  used, for microservice deployment 109
context map
  about 58, 59
  anticorruption layer 61
  conformist 61
  customer-supplier 60
  distillation 62
  open host service 62
  separate ways 61
  shared kernel 60
Continuous Deployment (CD) 8
Continuous Integration (CI) 8
correlation ID
  used, for tracking request 230
  using, for service calls 230
cyclic dependencies
  about 230
  analysis, while designing system 231
  different versions, maintaining 231
  impact 231

D

data access objects (DAO) 3
directives
  ng-app 164
  ng-bind 164
  ng-model 164
  ng-repeat 164
  ng-submit 164
Docker
  4 GB memory 109
  about 13
  architecture 13
  configuration 109
  containers, managing 117, 118
  image 14

55287502R00144

Made in the USA
Lexington, KY
19 September 2016